I0426951

To the explorers of imaginary worlds and enthusiasts of vibrant art, this book is dedicated to you. May the pages within inspire your creativity and transport you to the magical realms of mythology. Let each stroke of color be a unique journey, filled with charm and discovery. May this coloring book bring joy, relaxation, and a special connection to myths that endure through the ages. May your creations be as extraordinary as the magic that lives within these pages. With gratitude and inspiration

Alan Cristian

2024

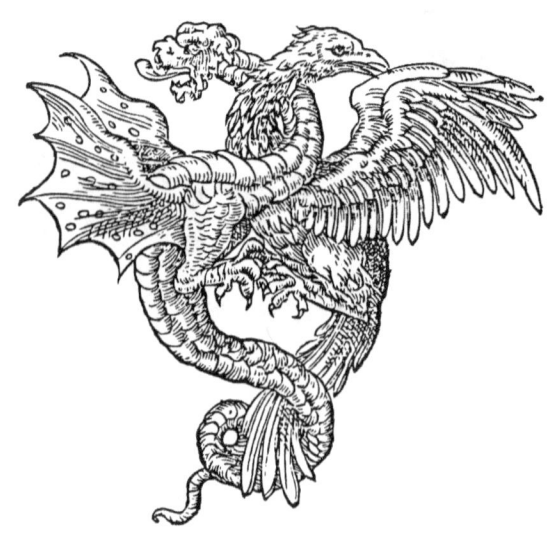

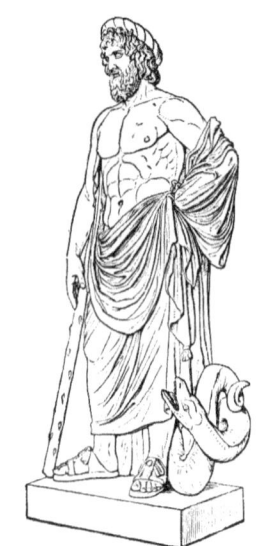

This Book Belongs to:

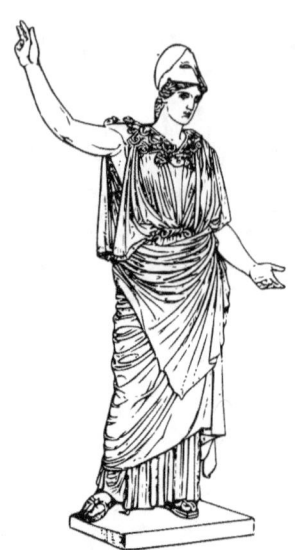

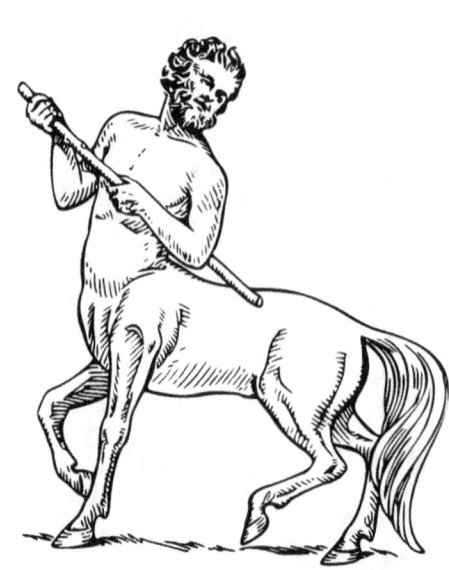

Test Color Page

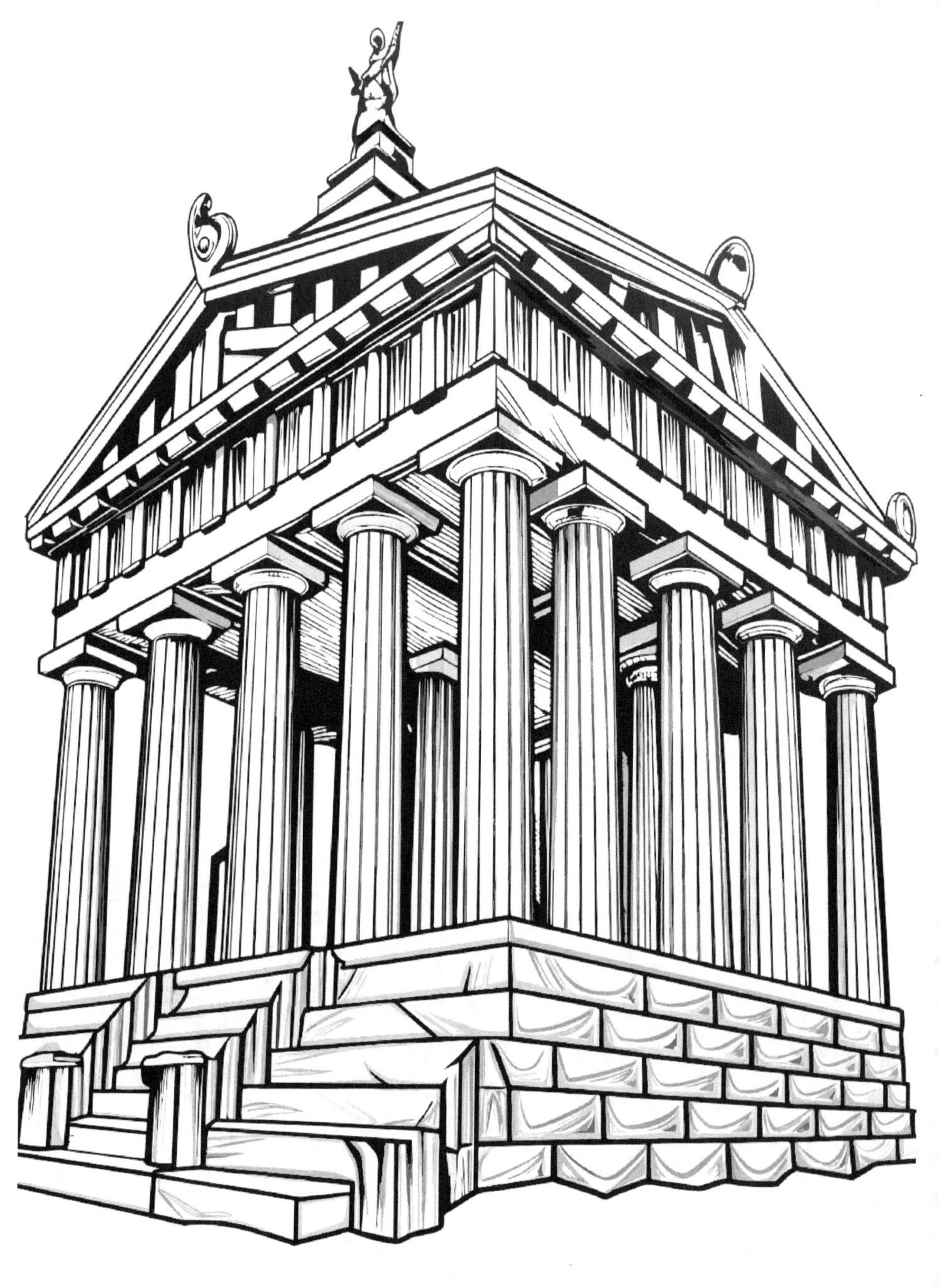

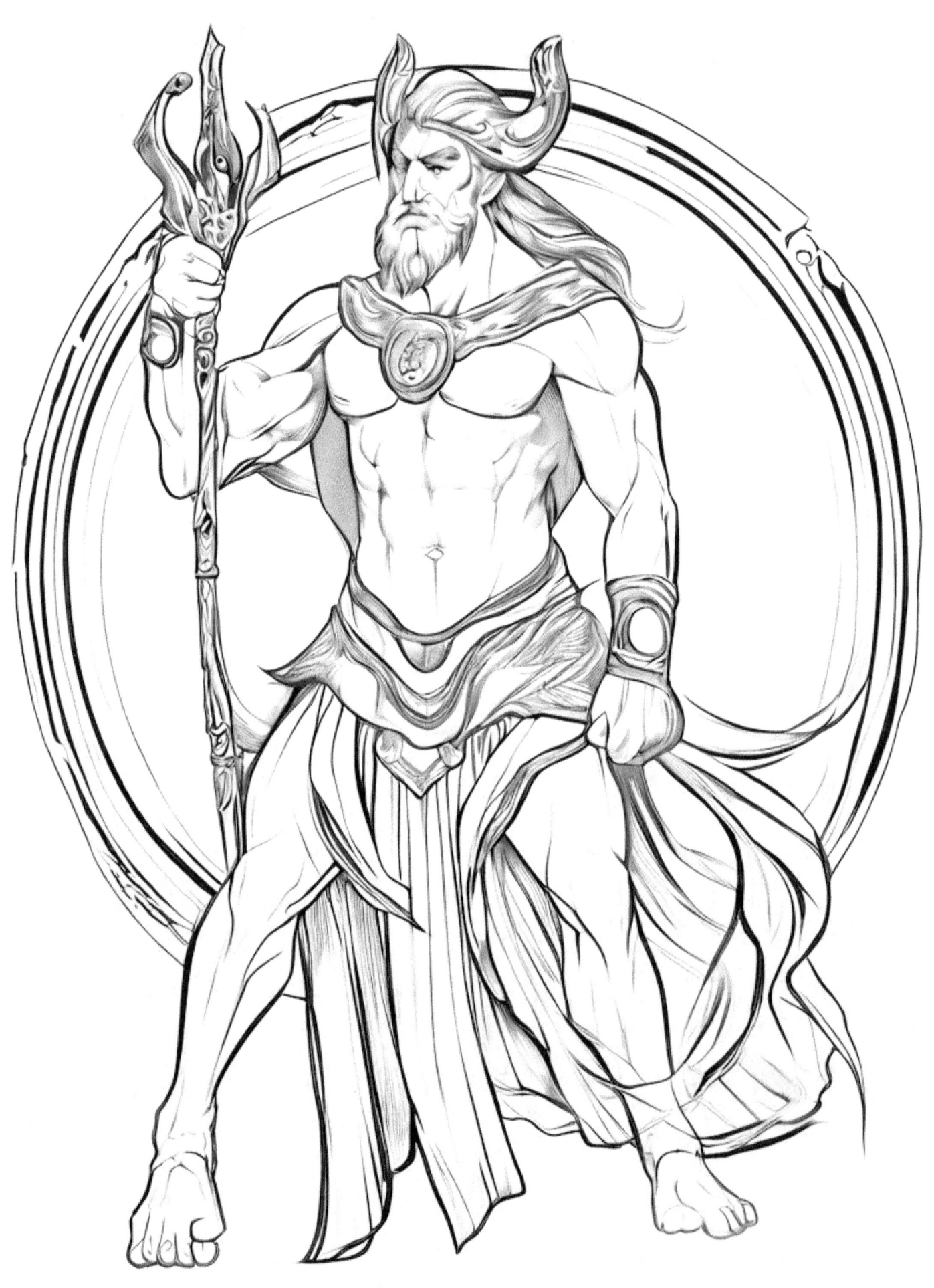

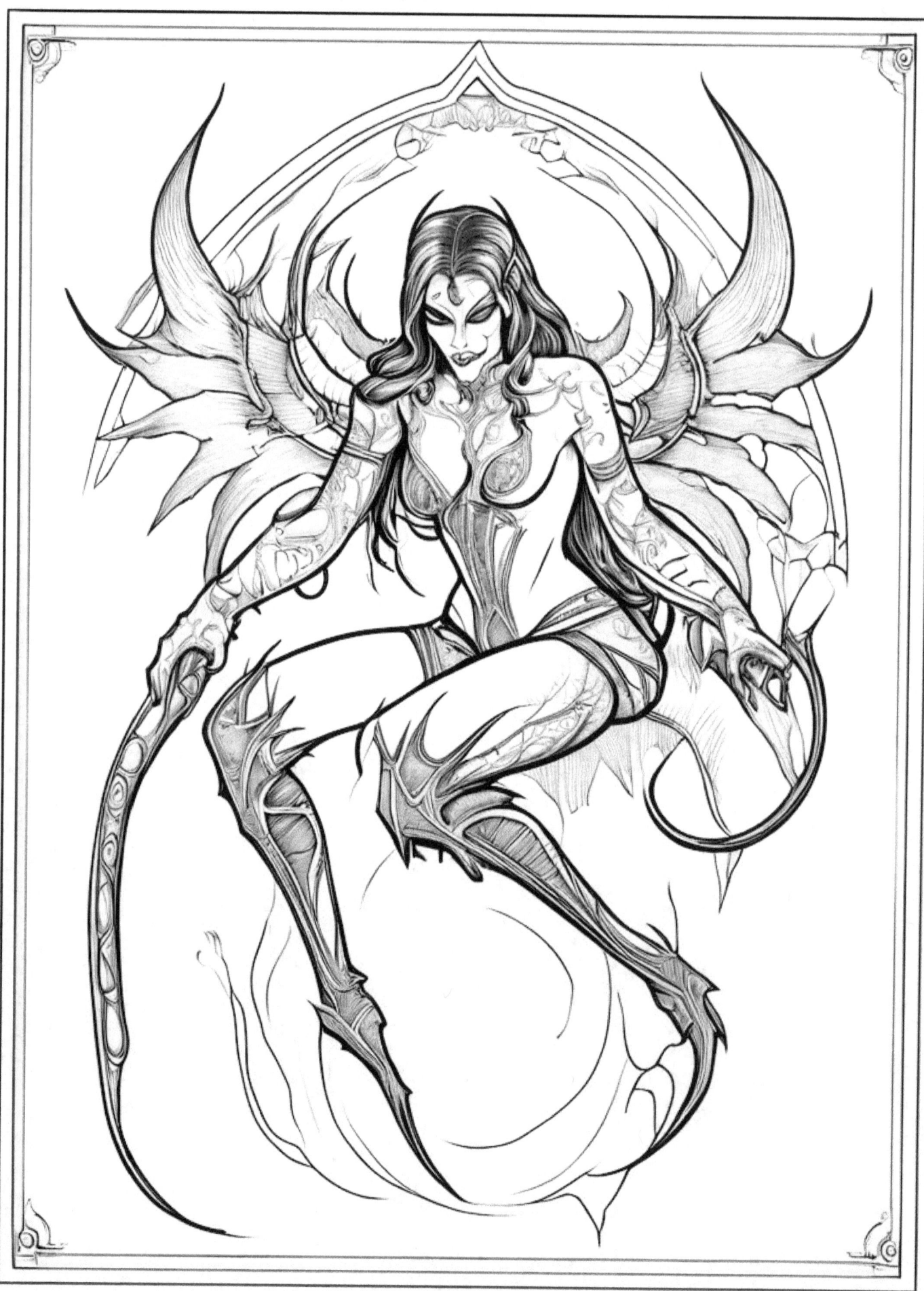

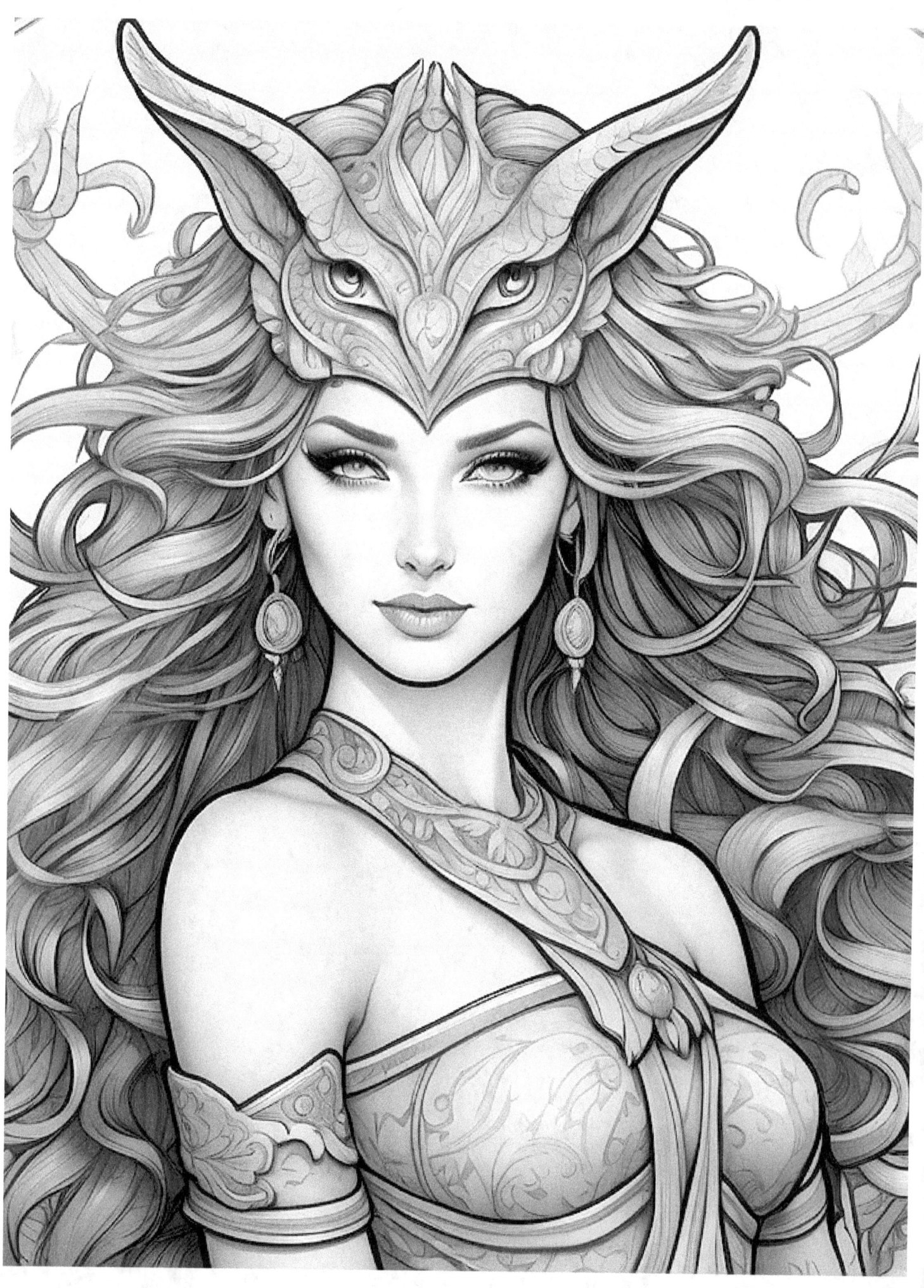

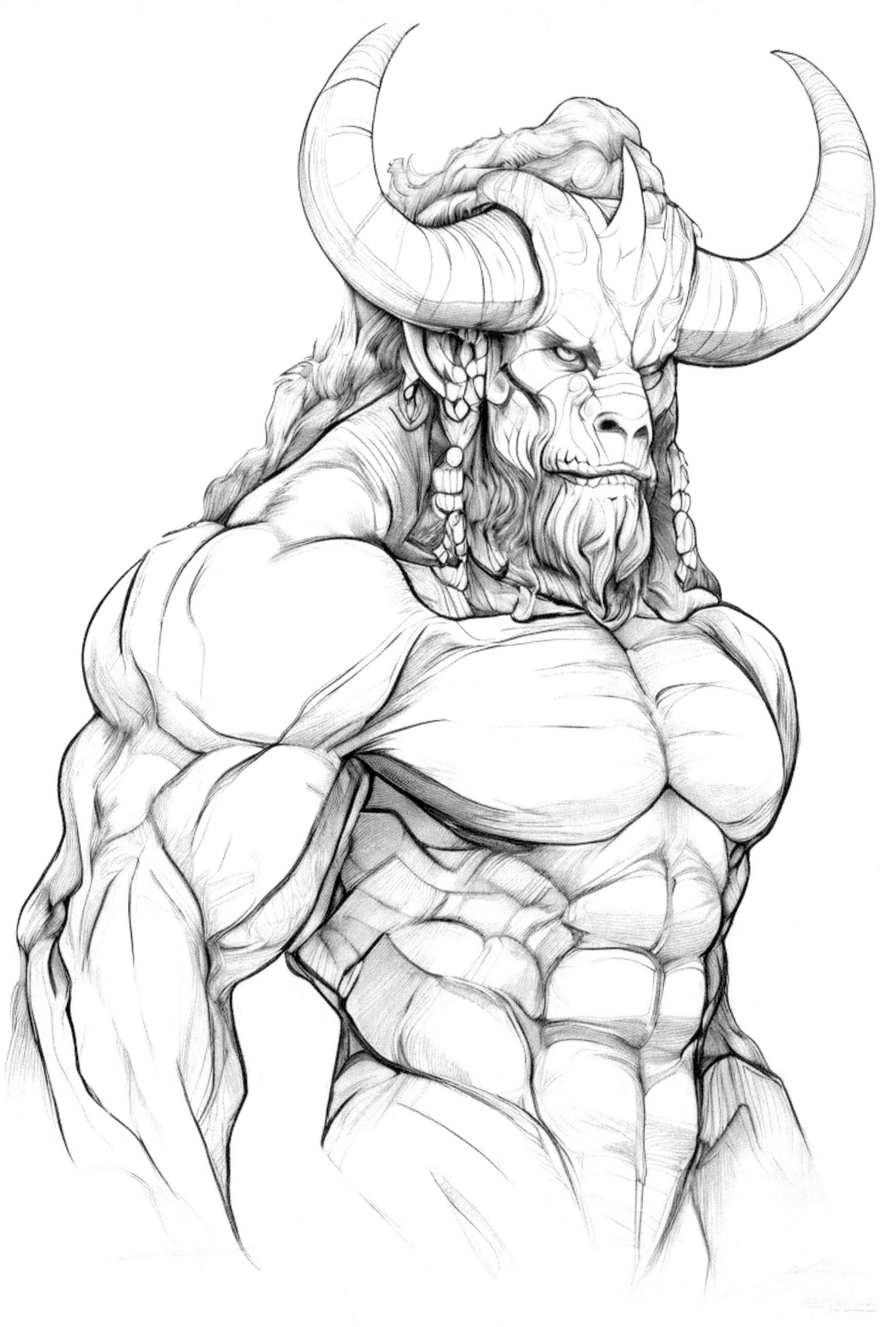

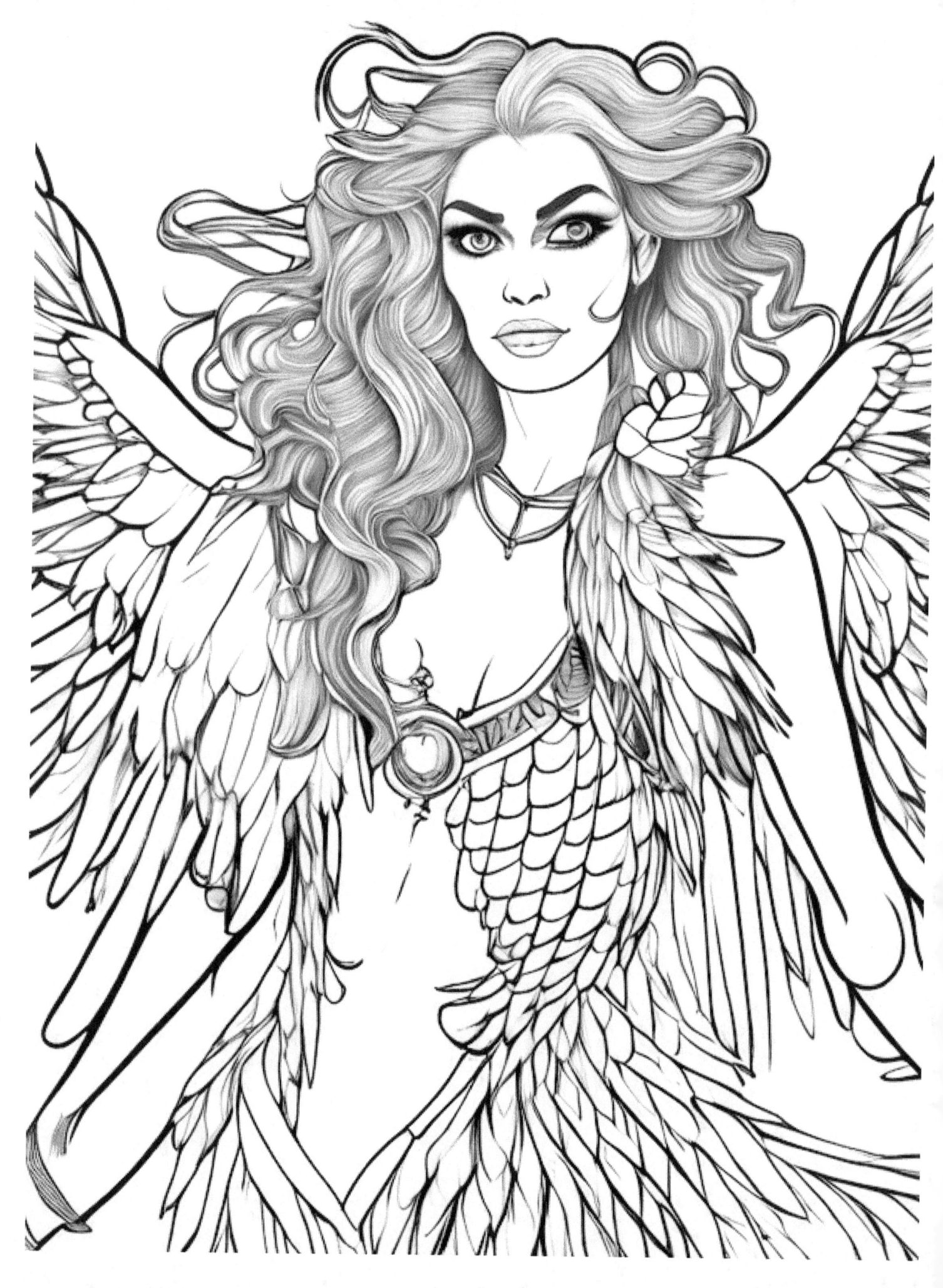

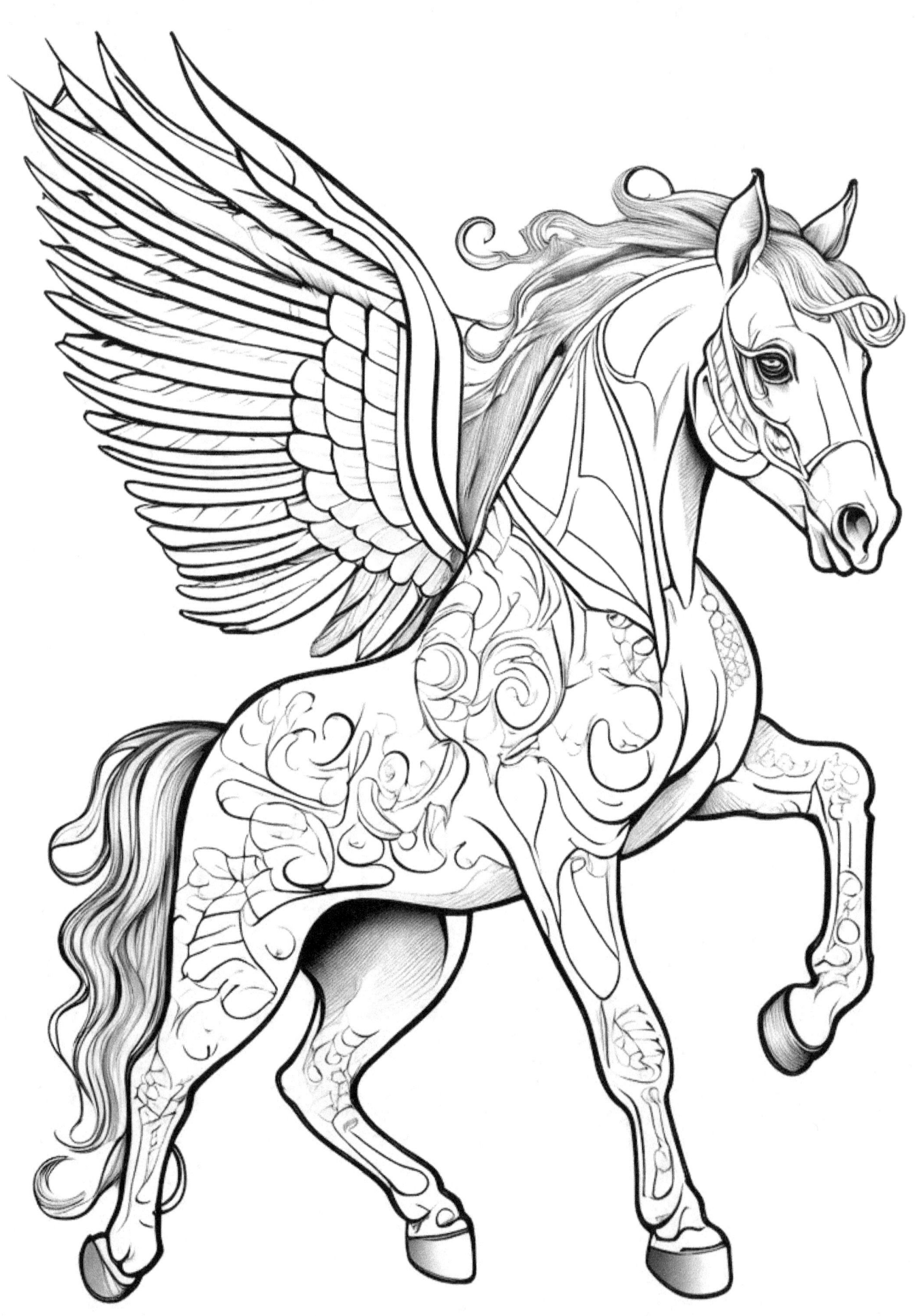

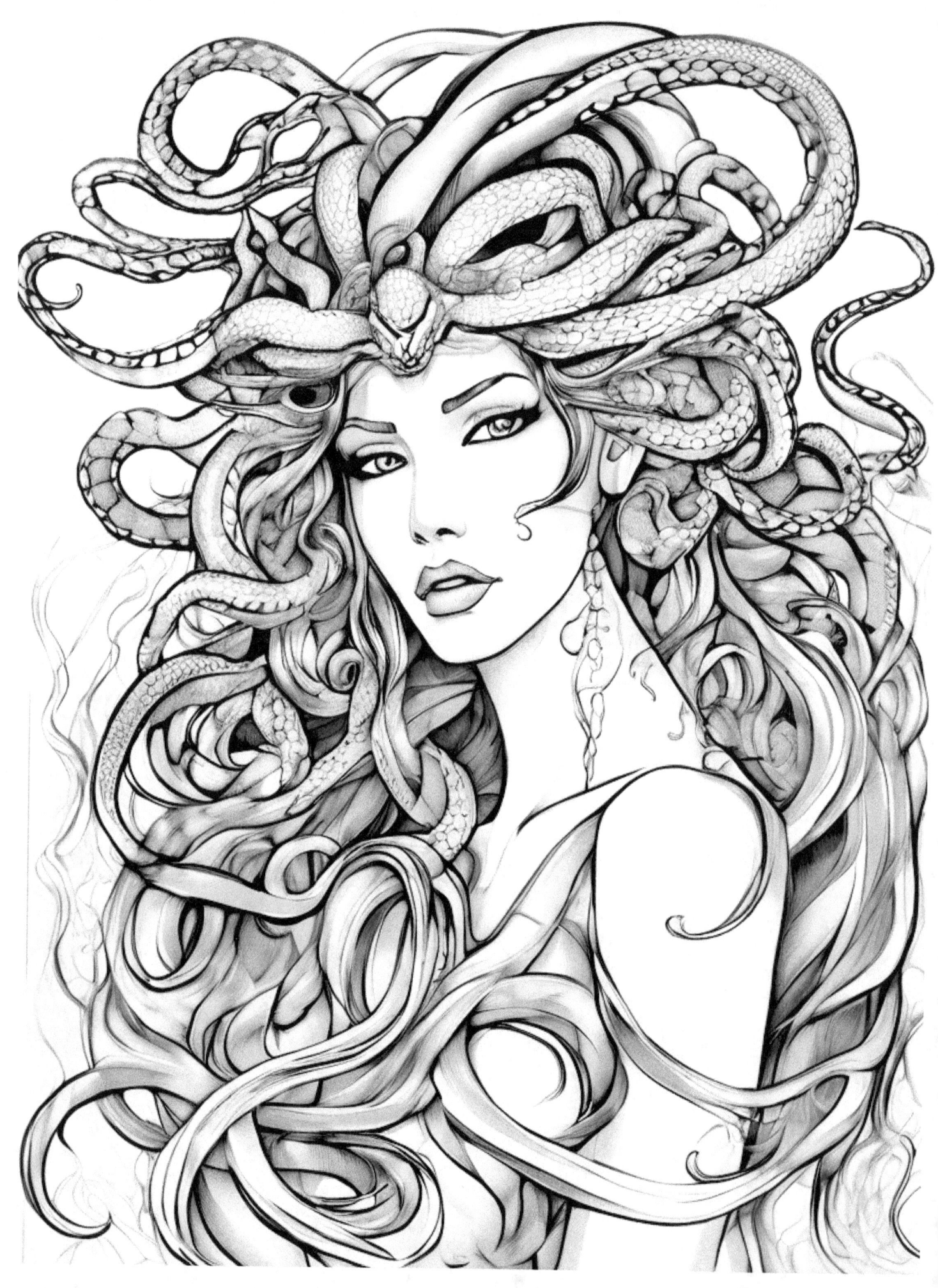

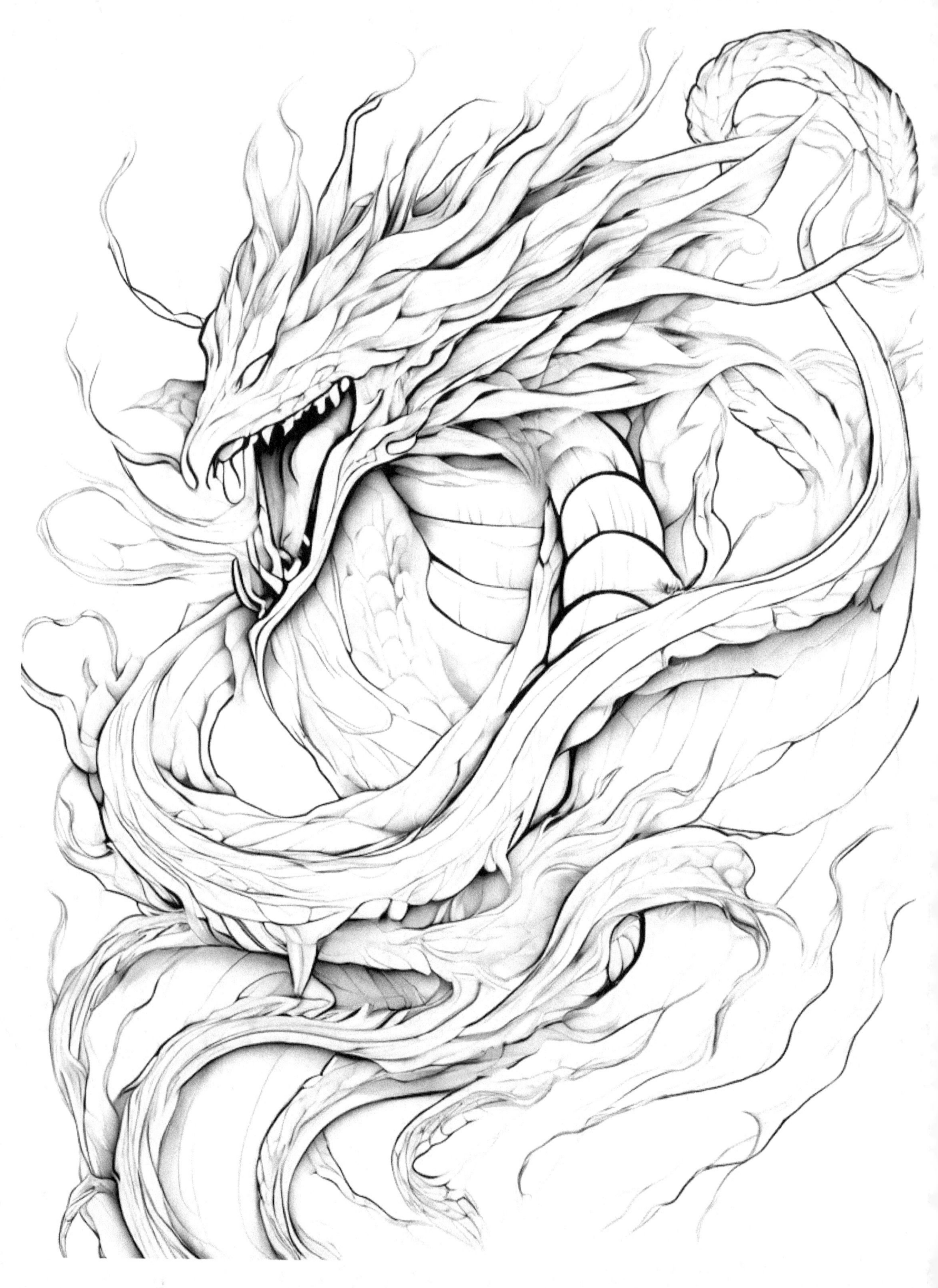

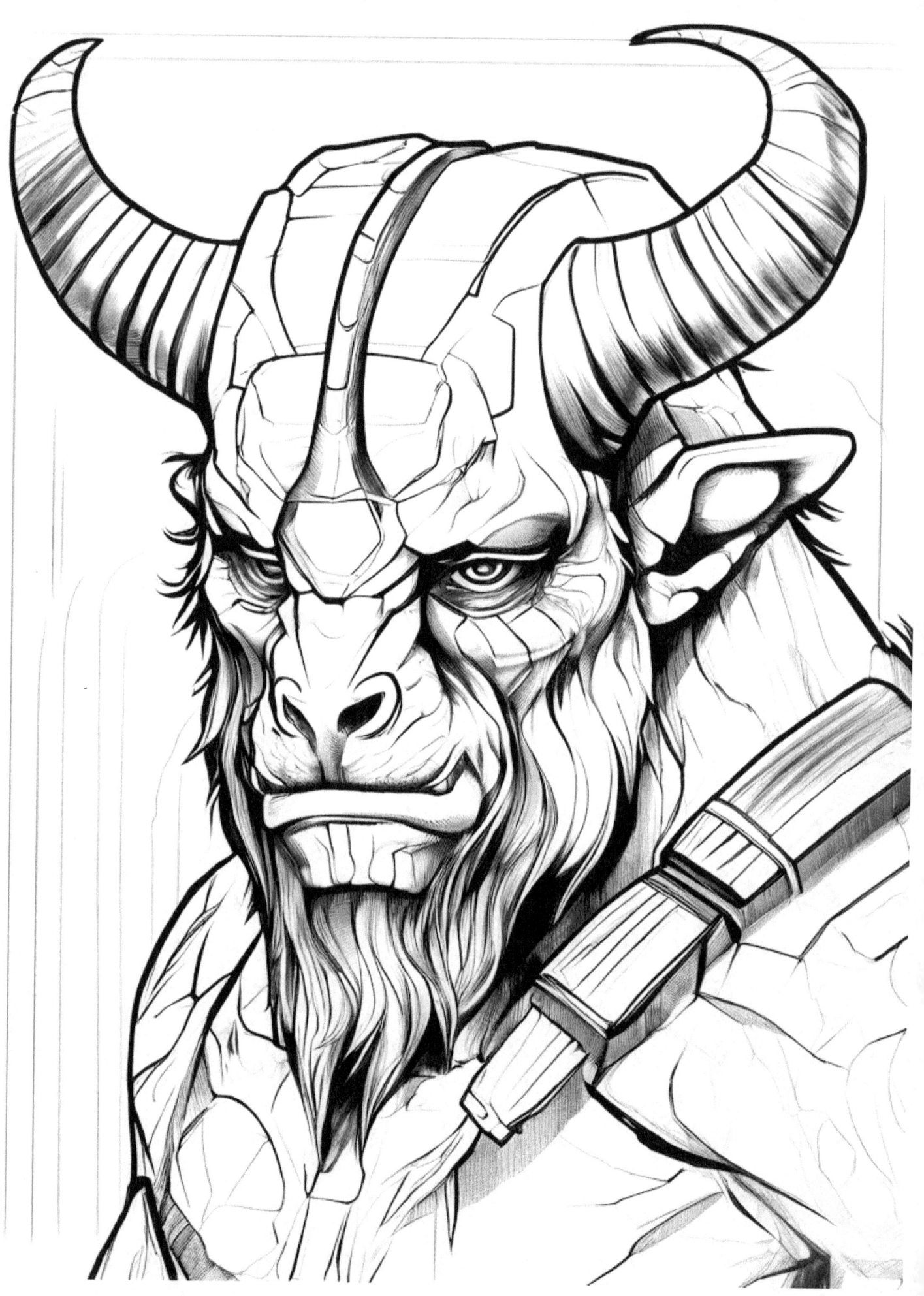

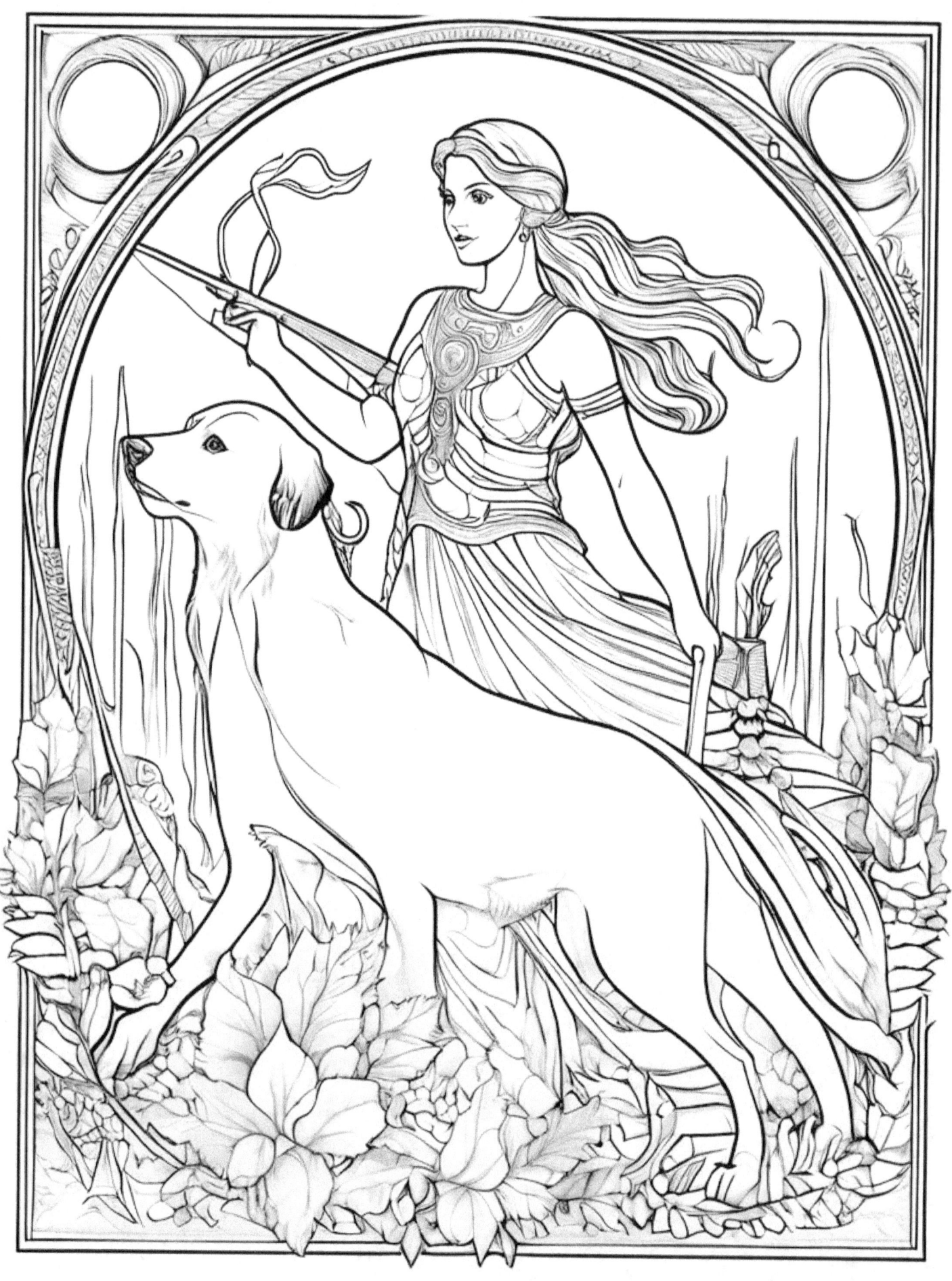

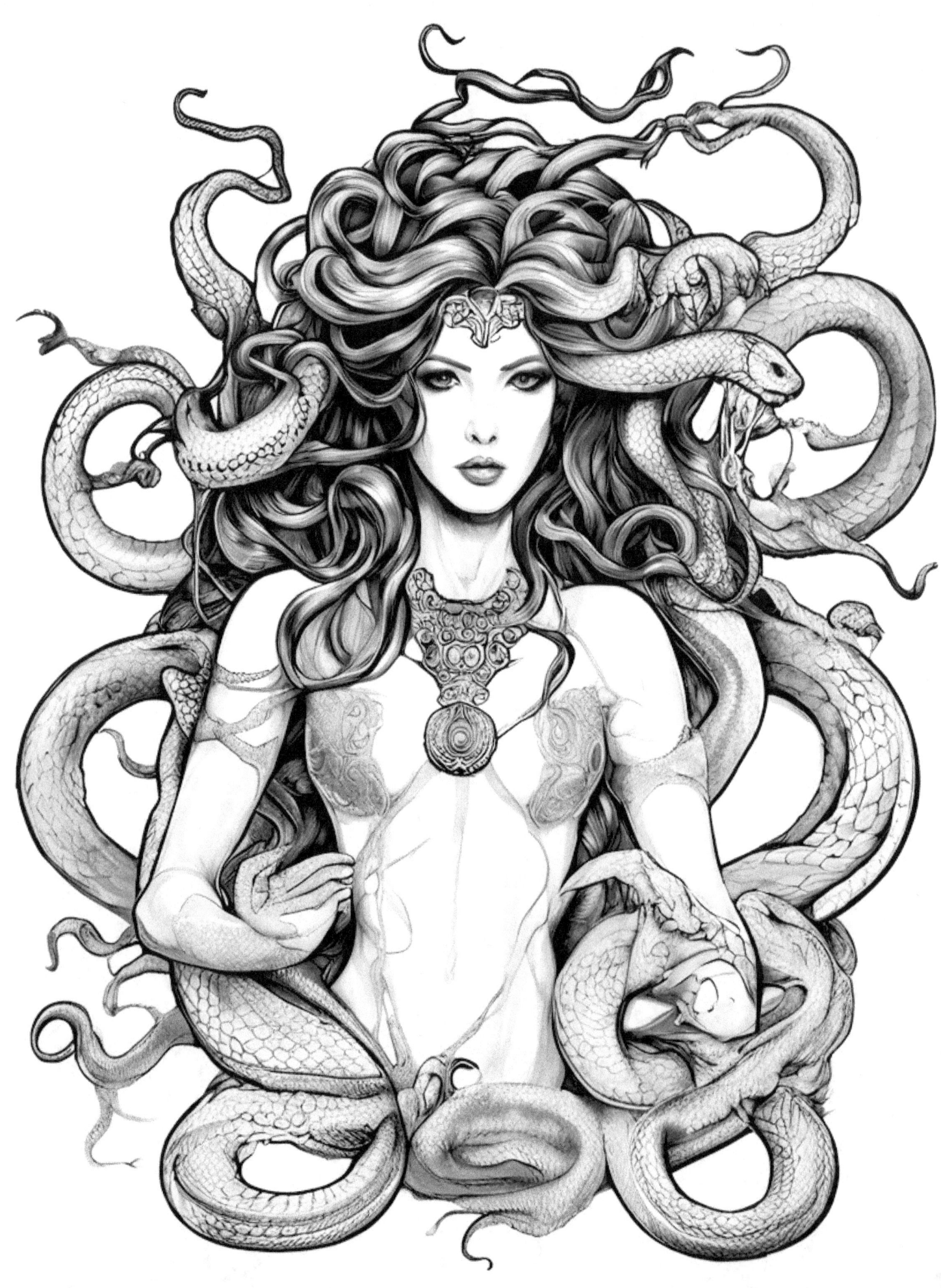

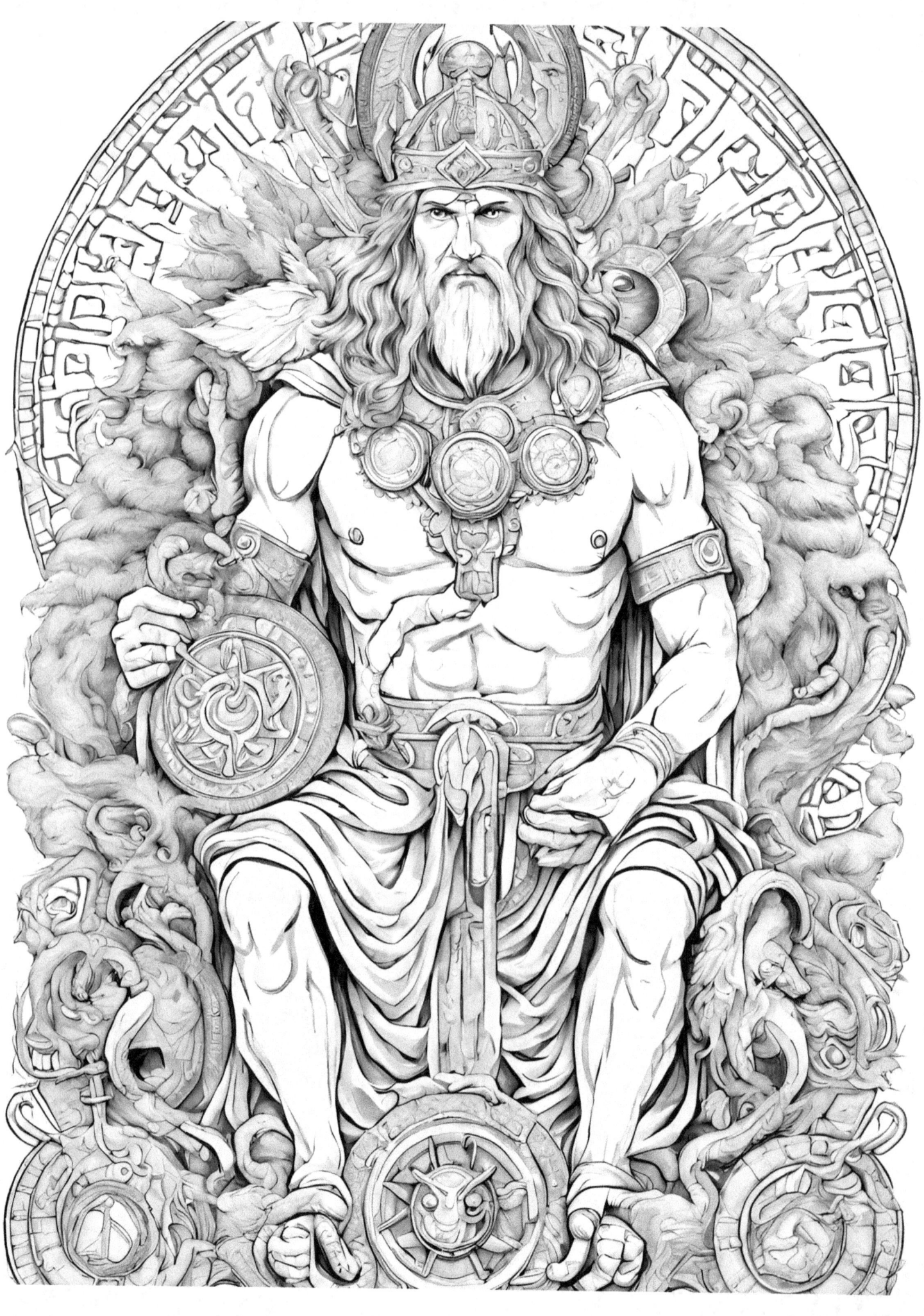

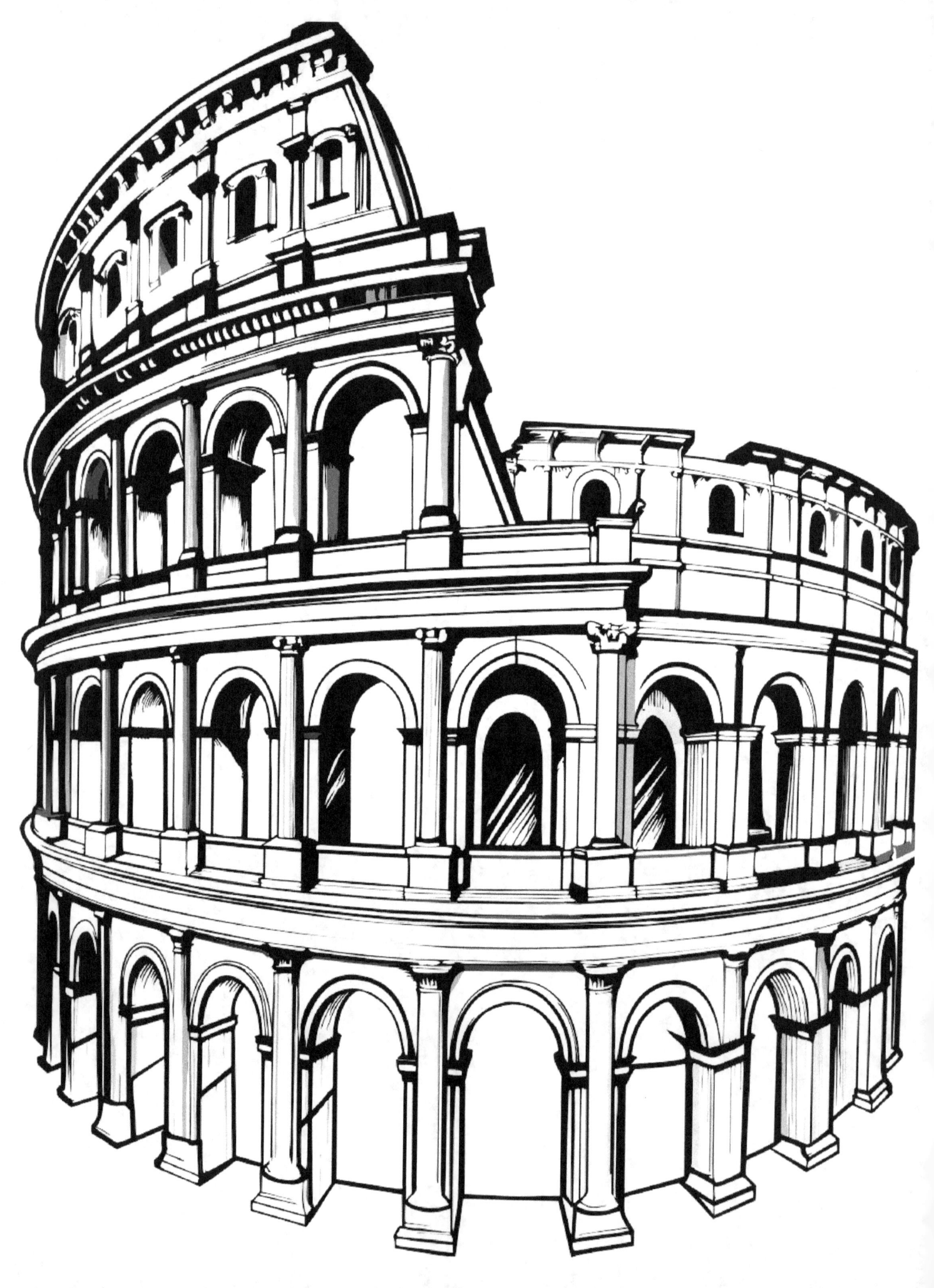

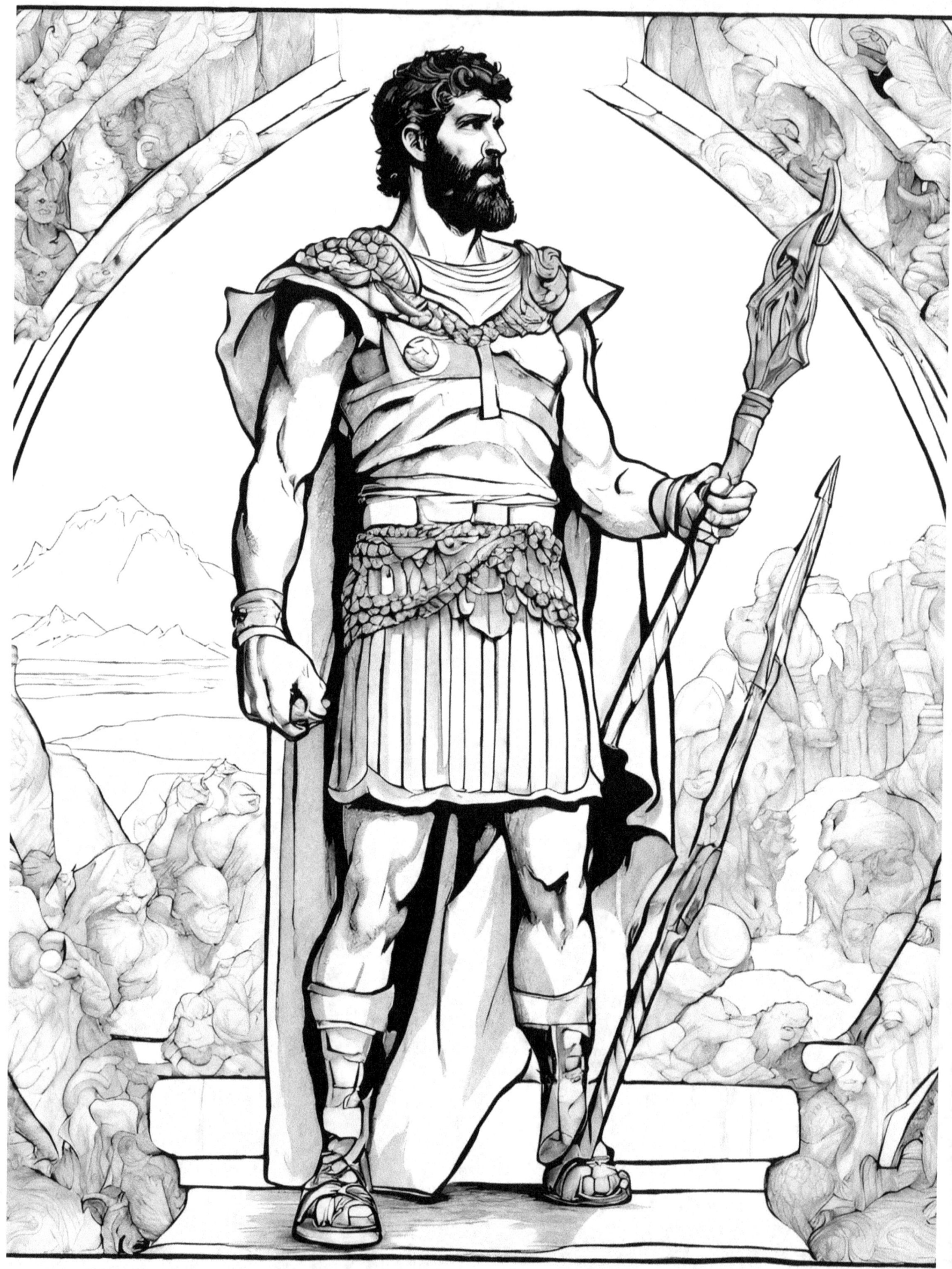

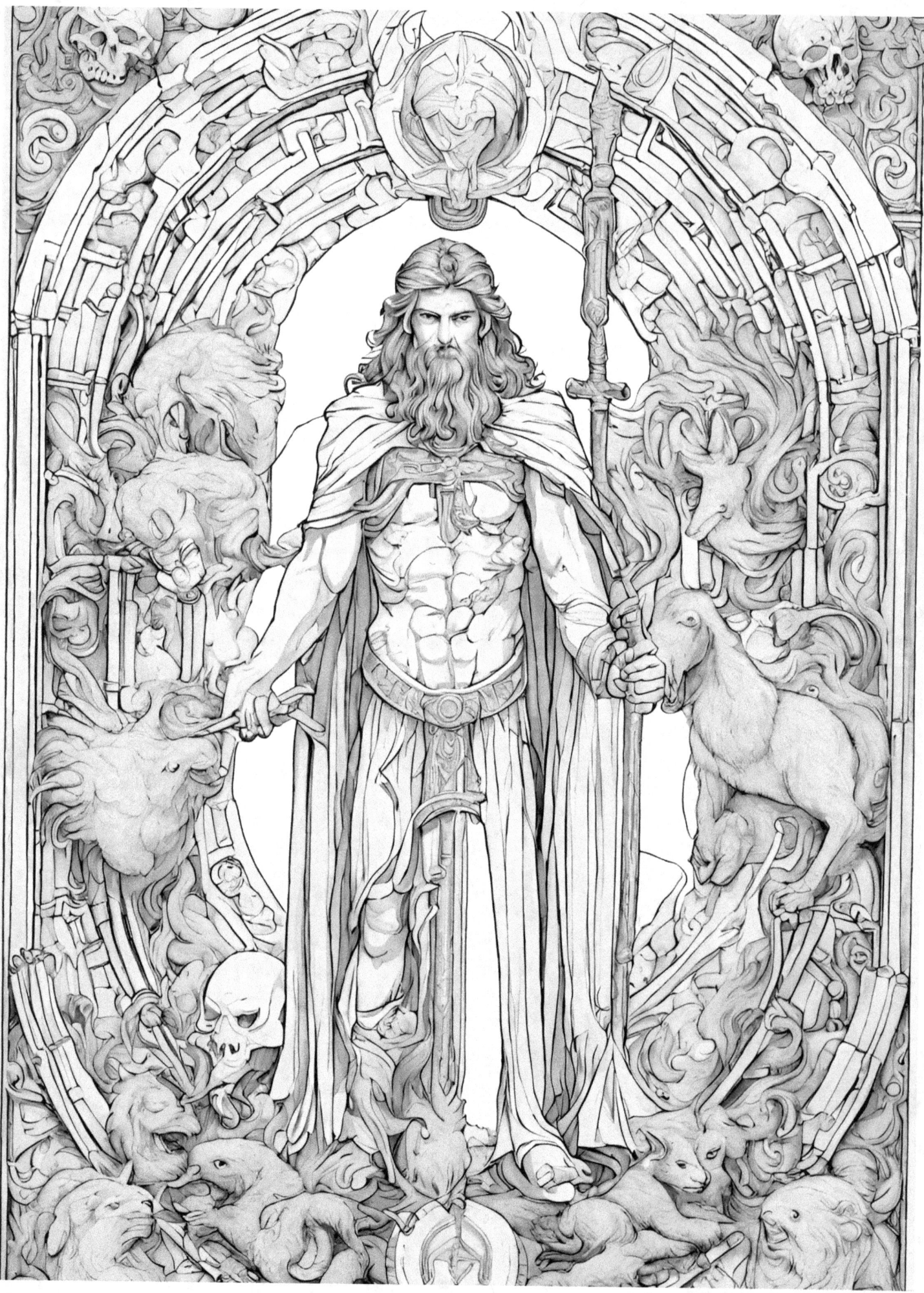

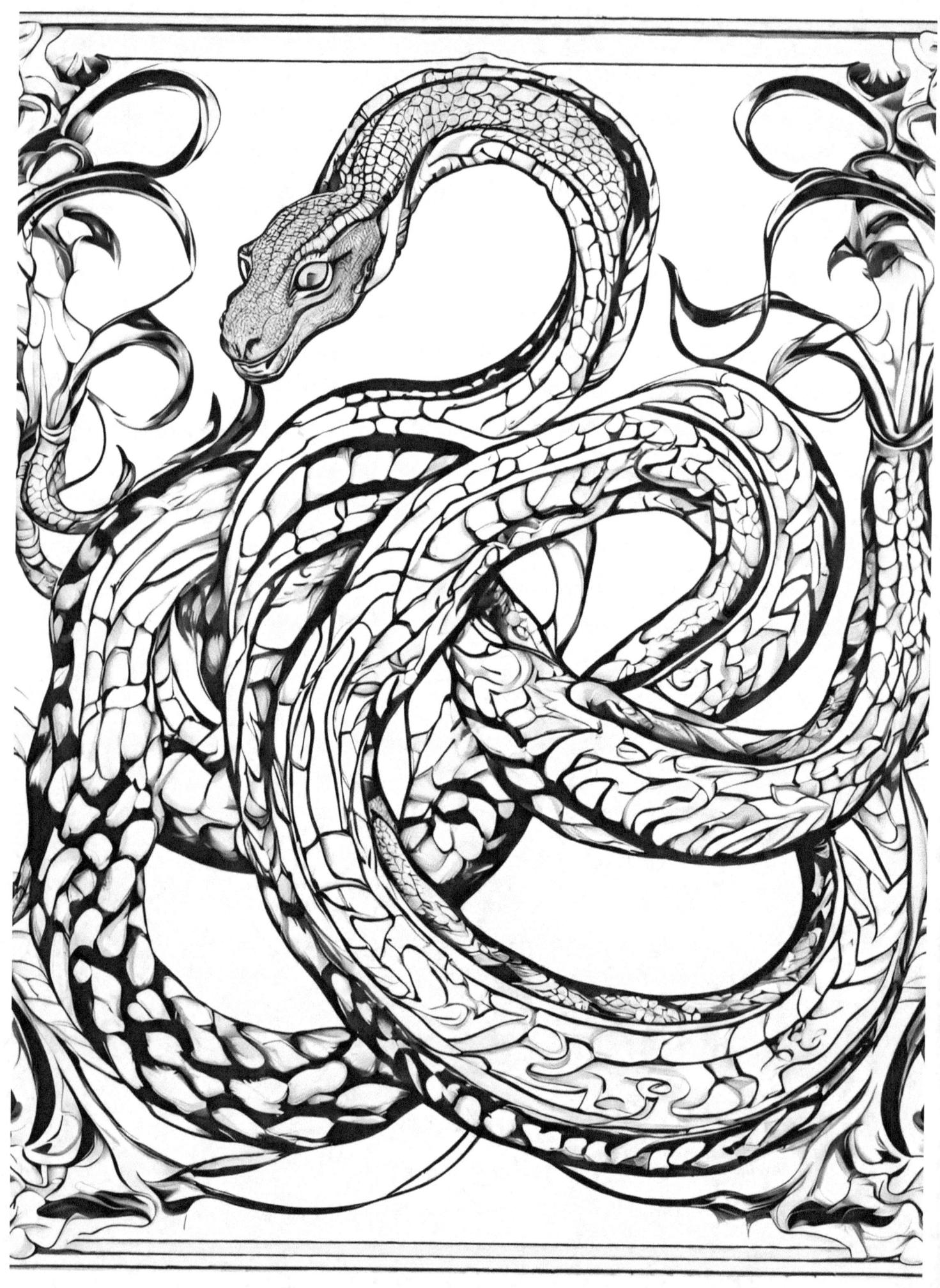

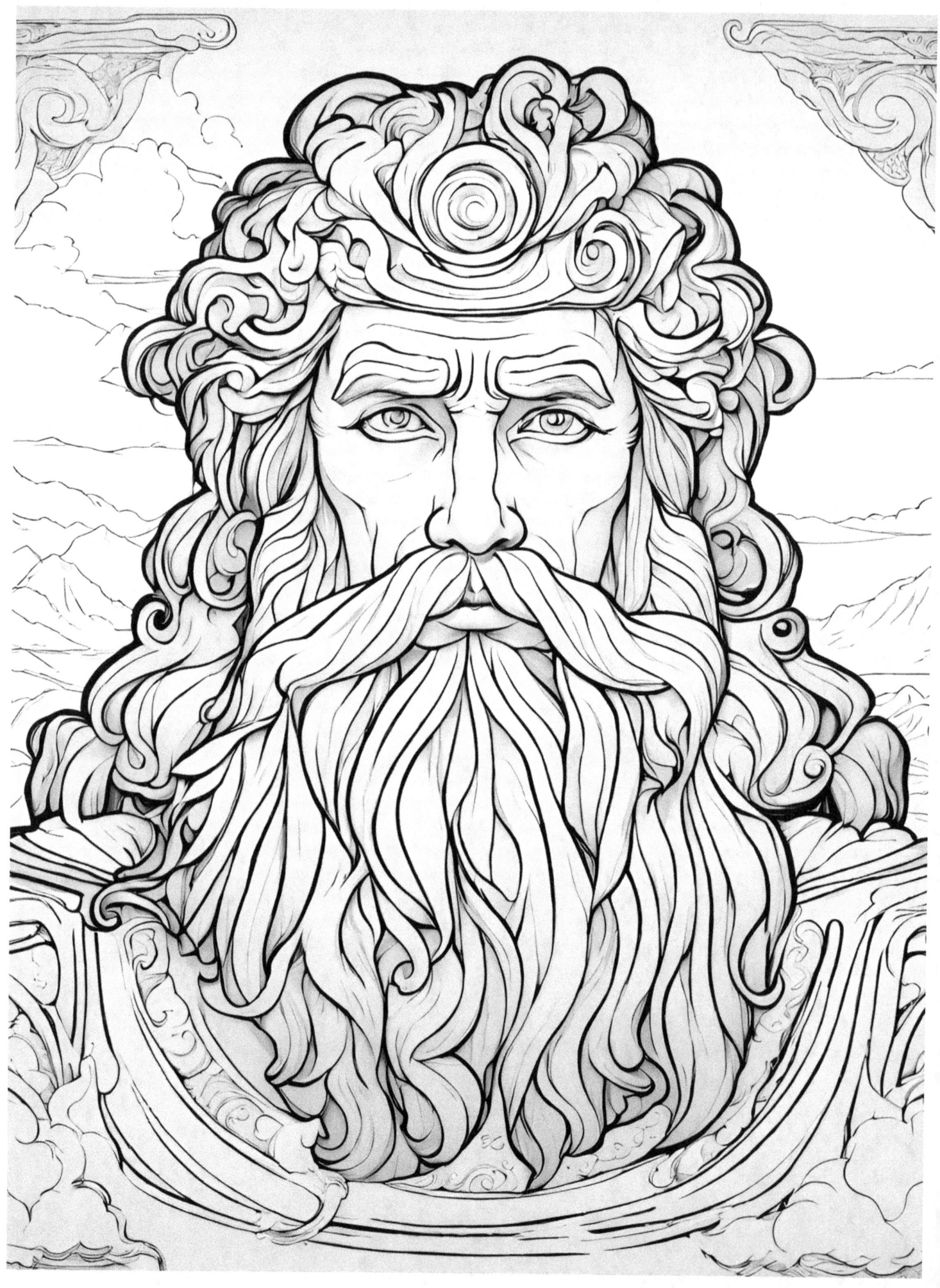

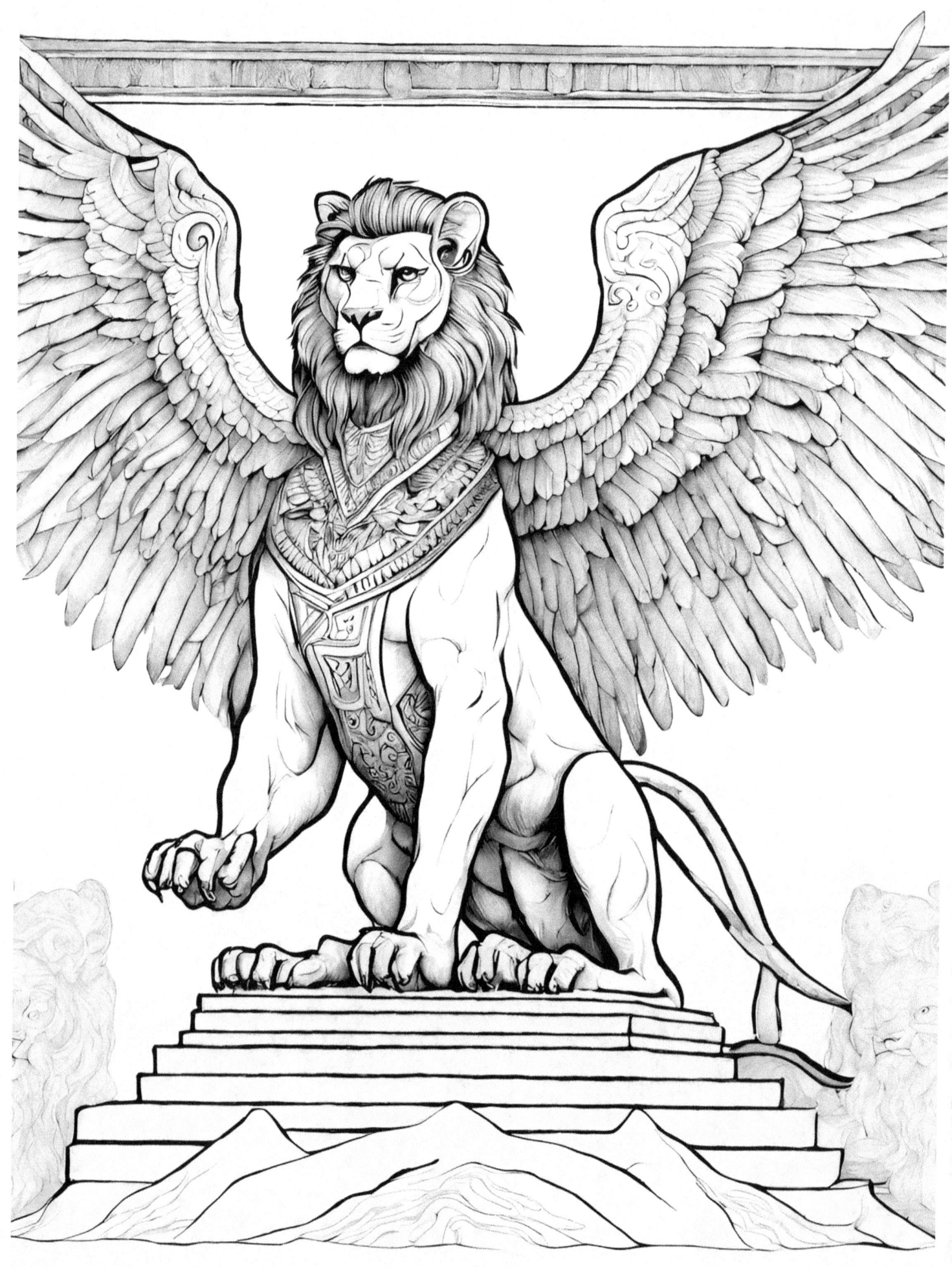

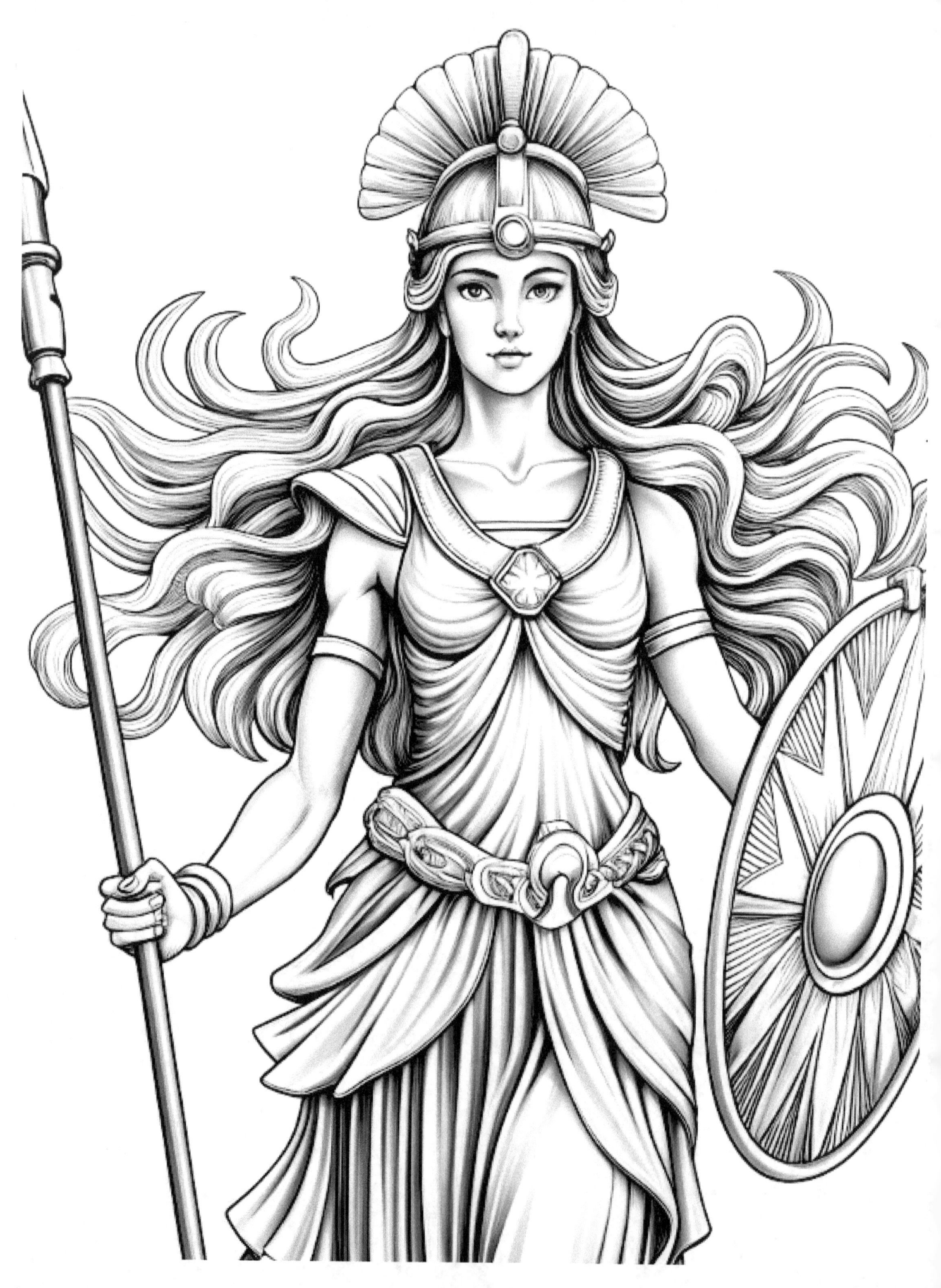

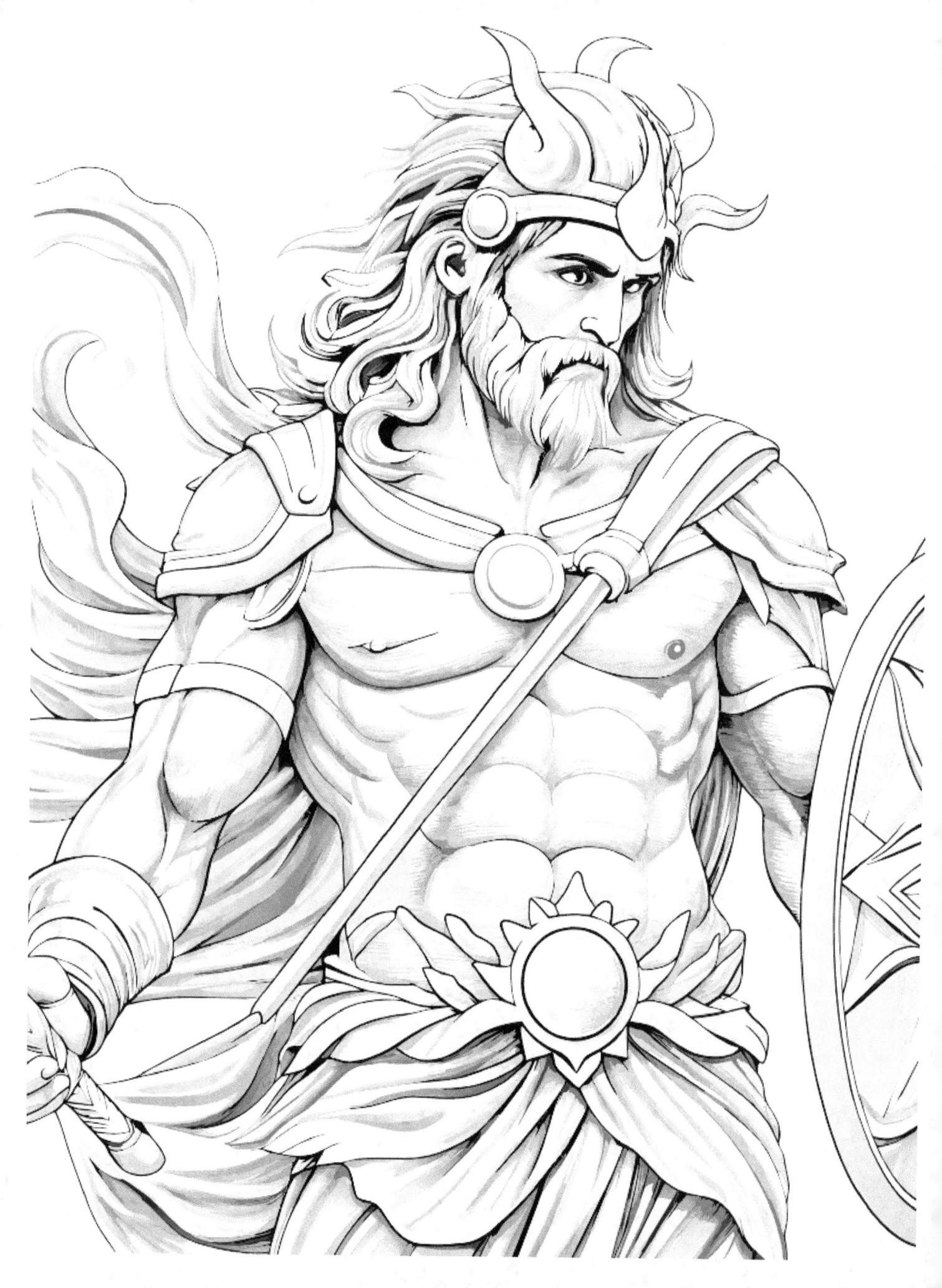

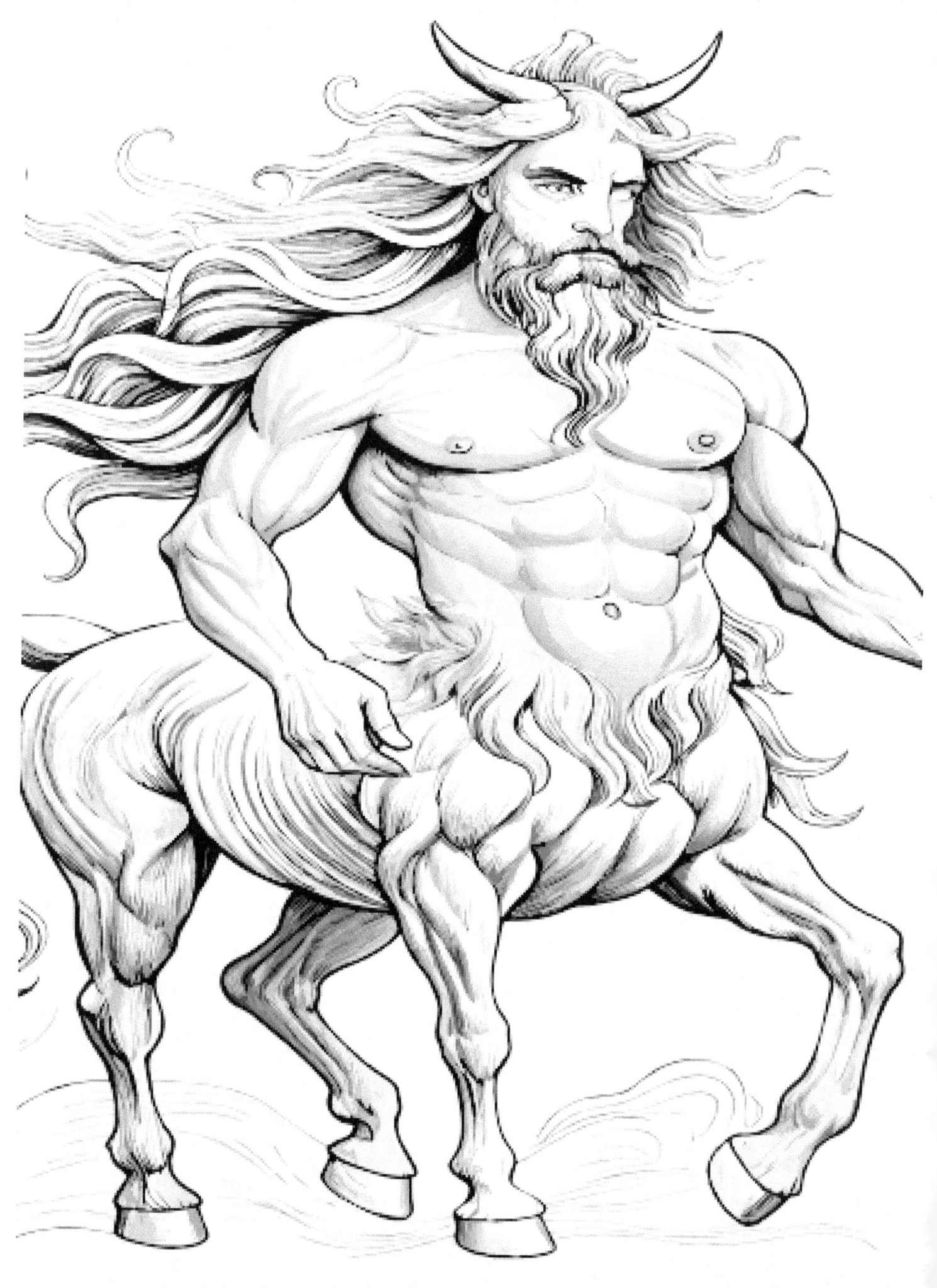

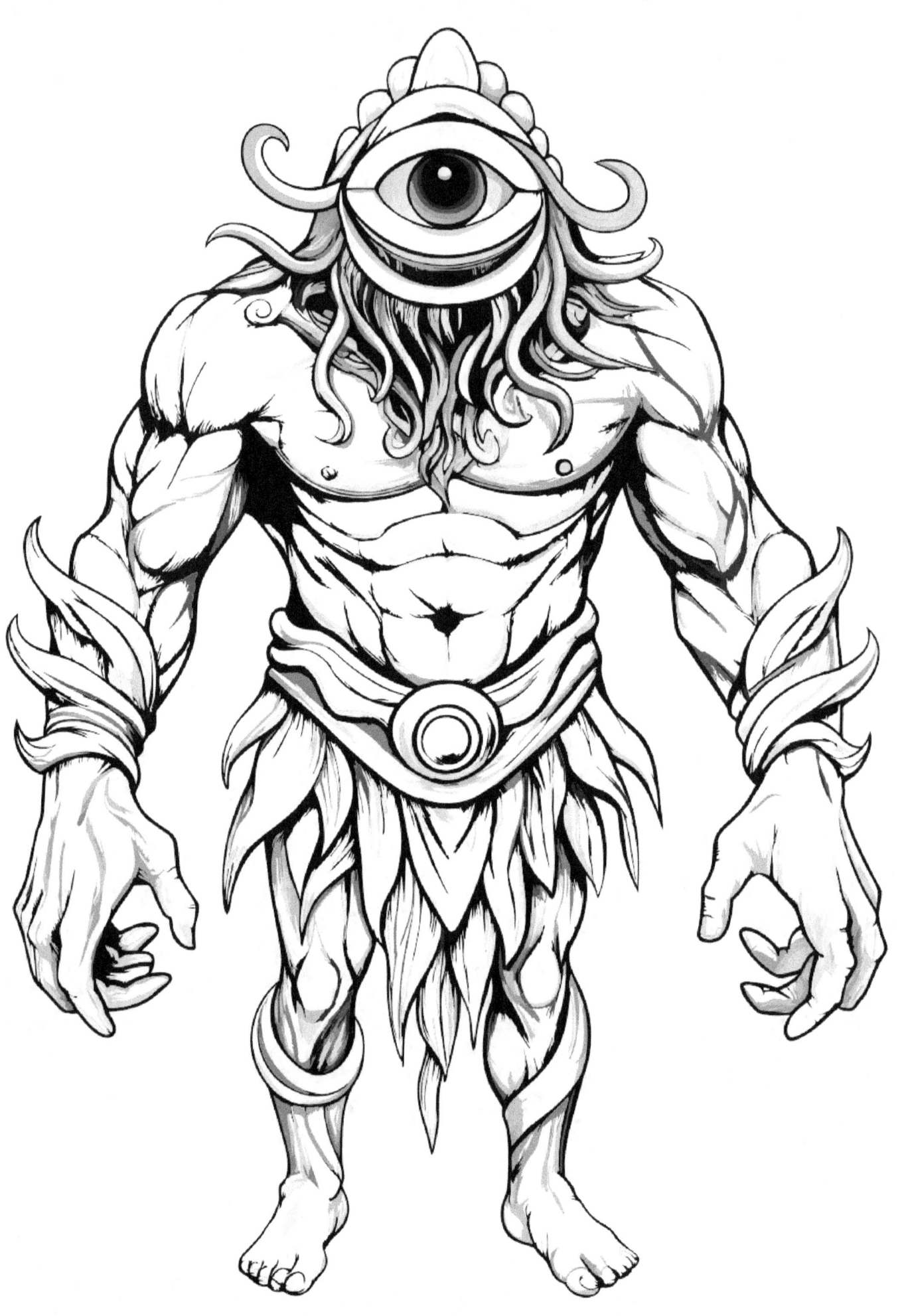

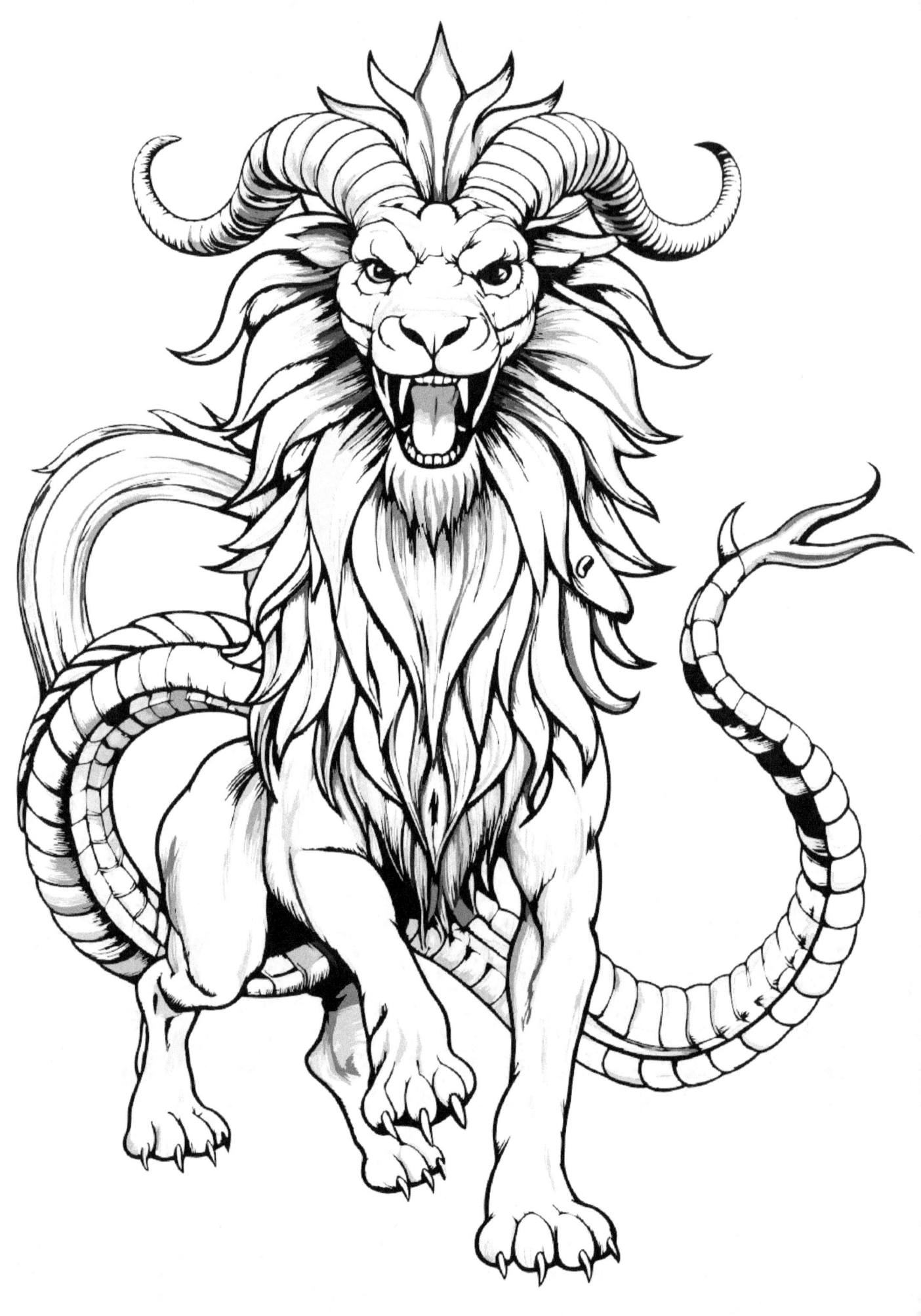

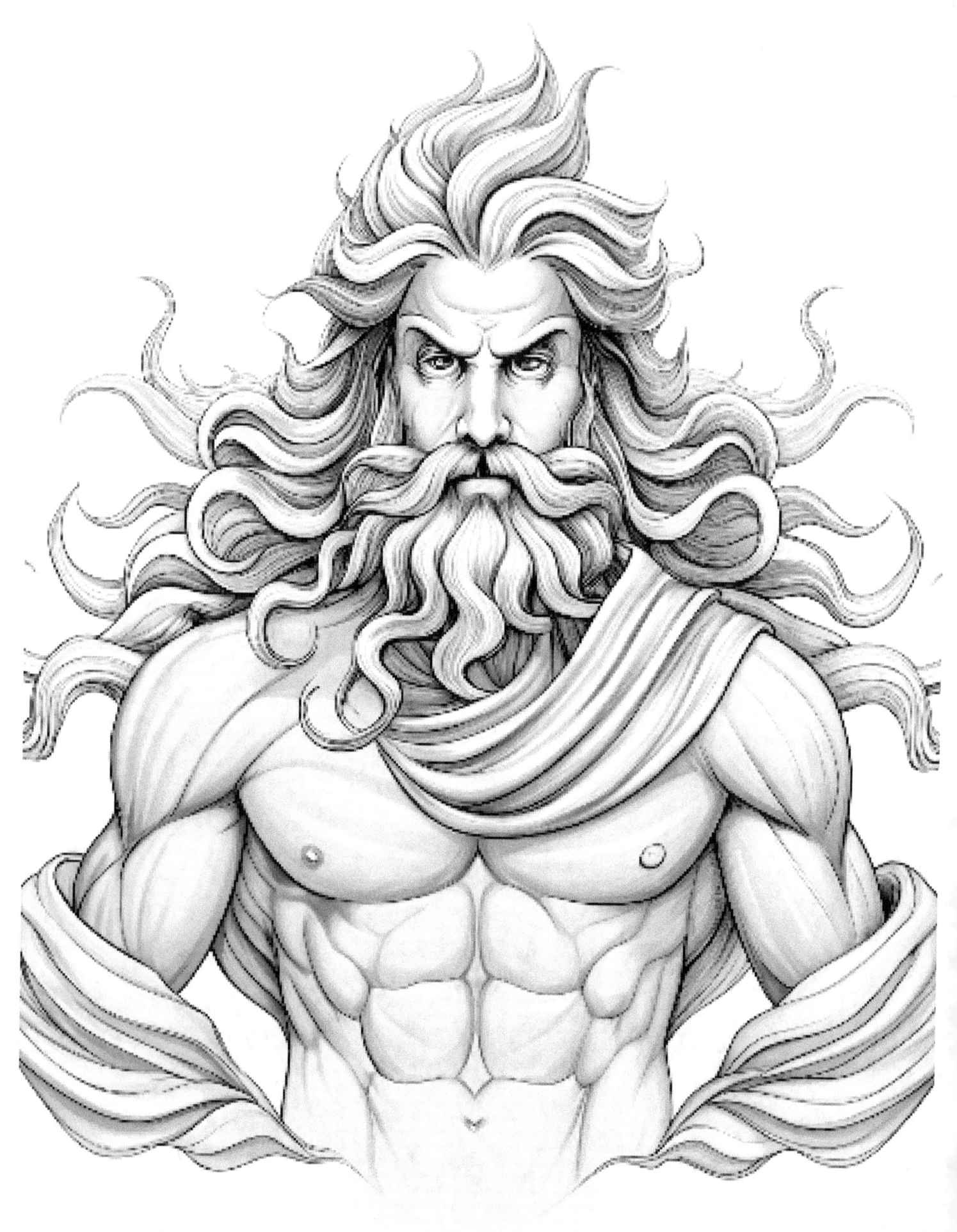

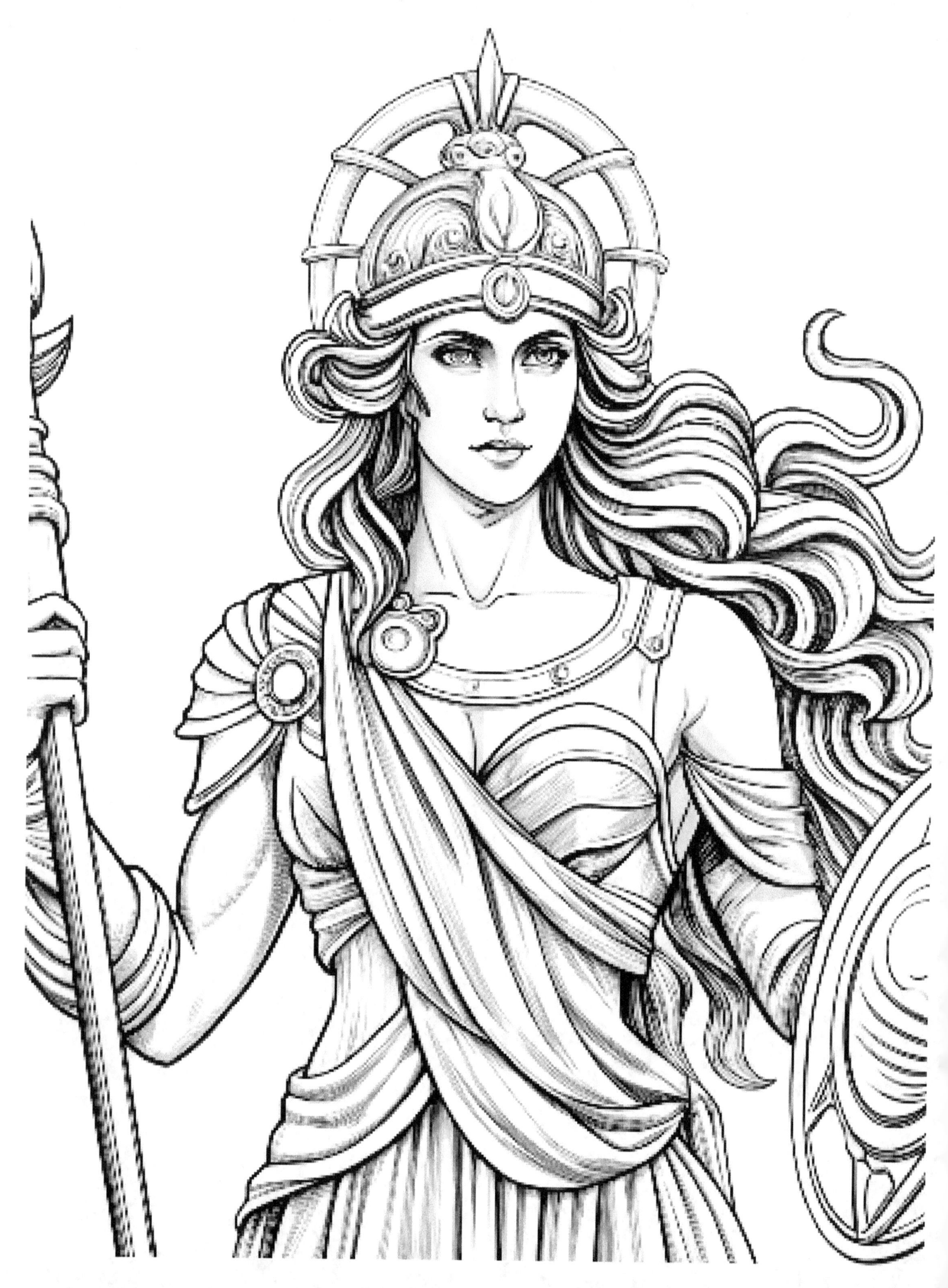

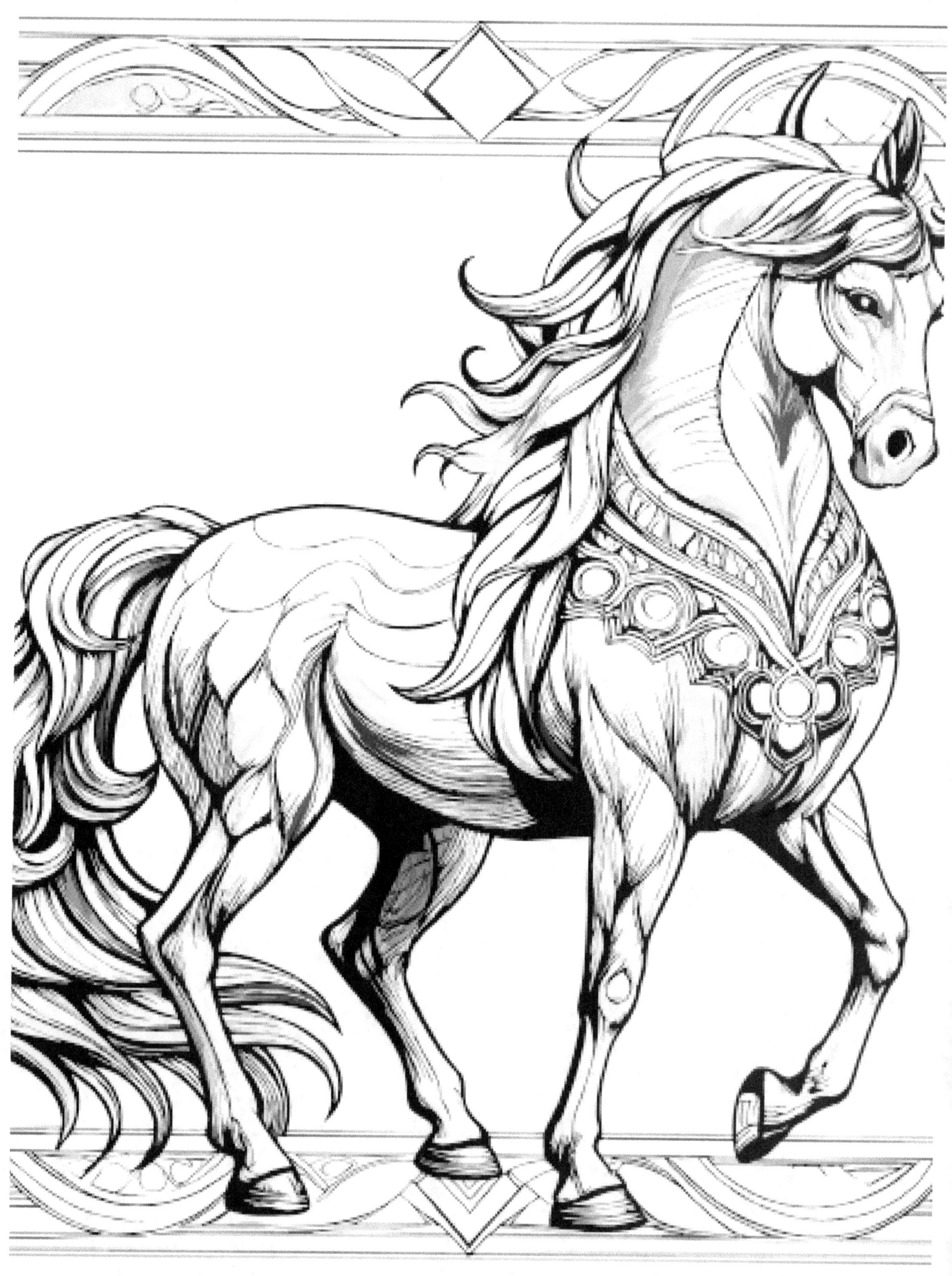

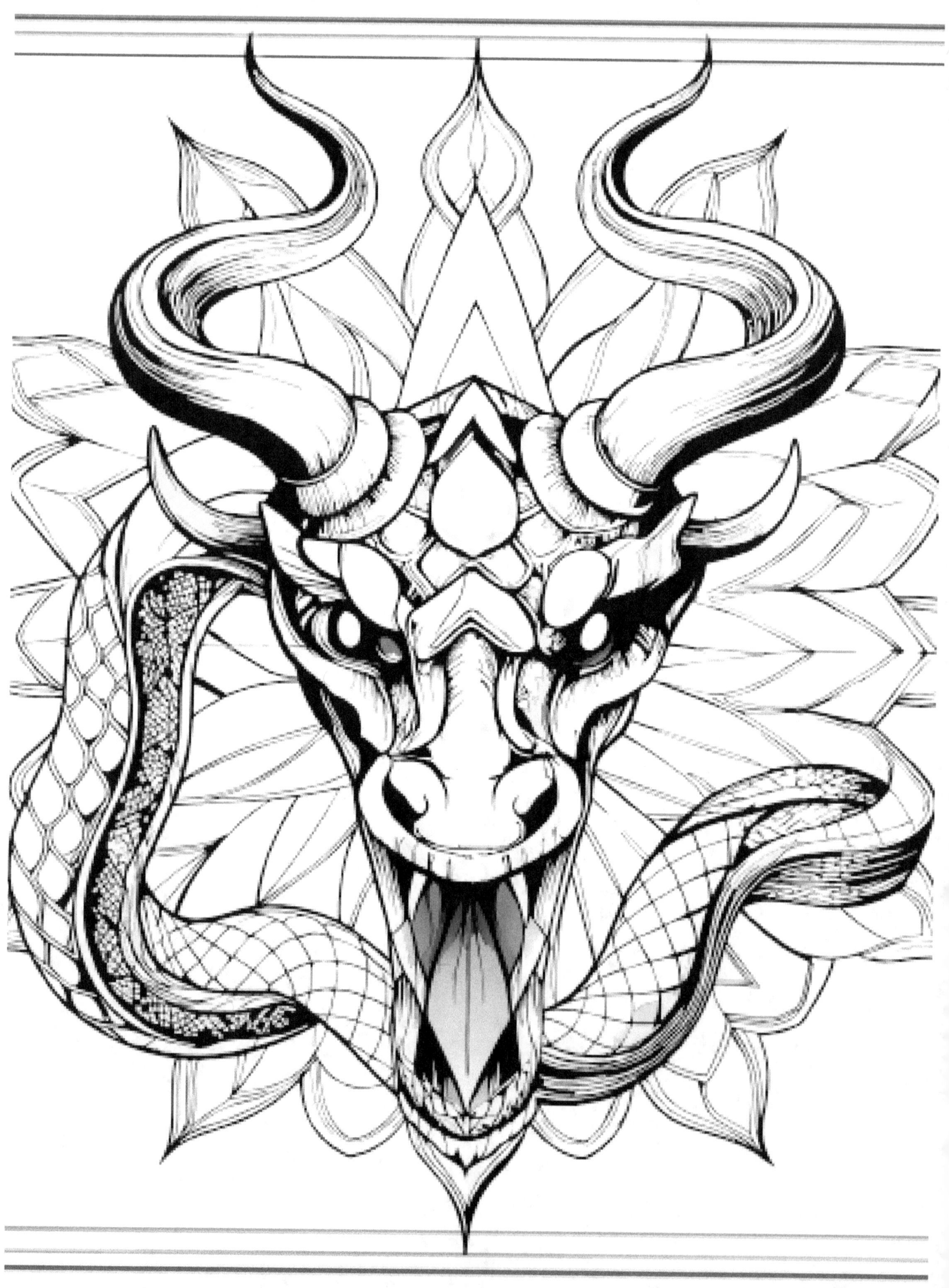

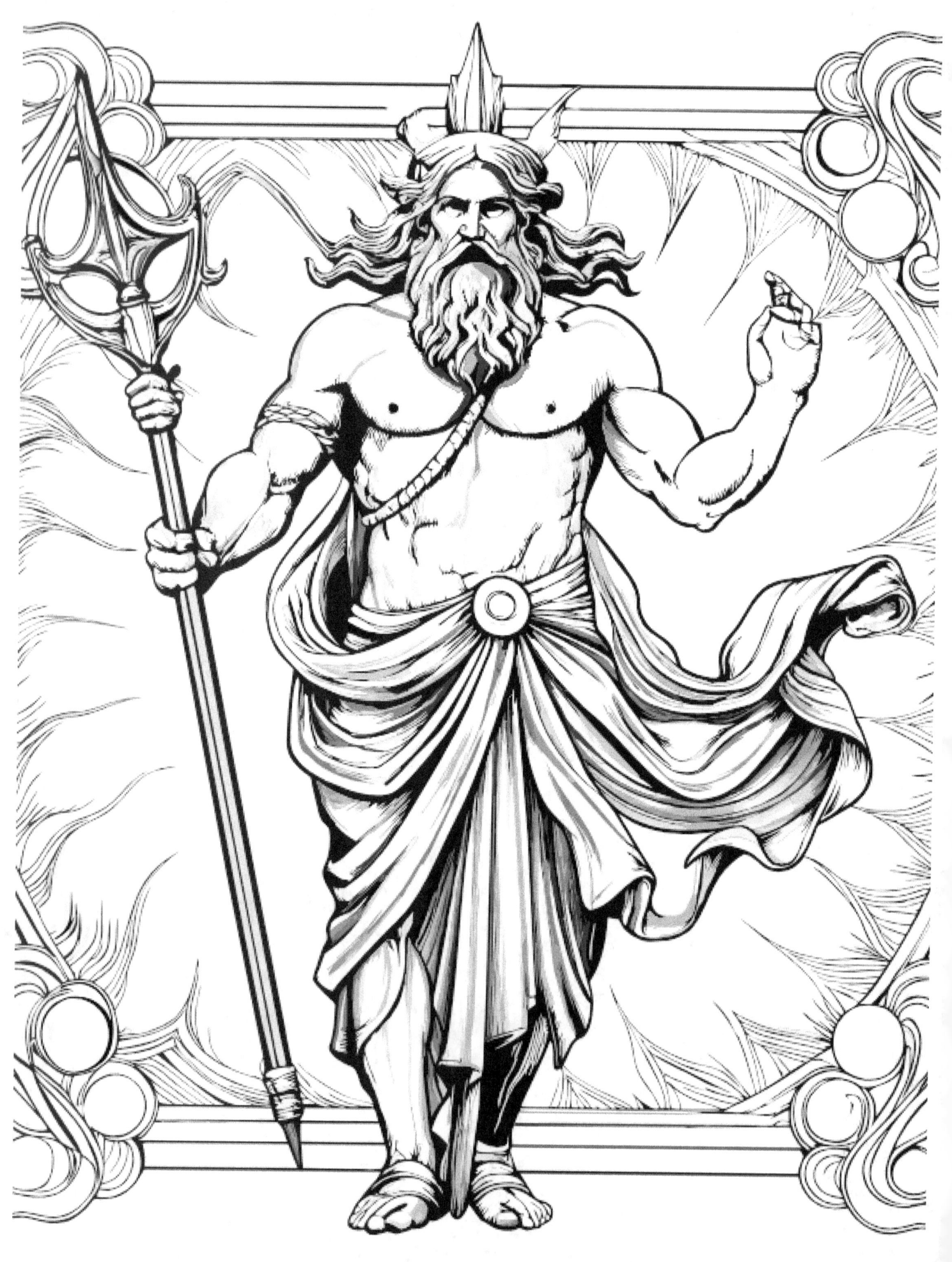

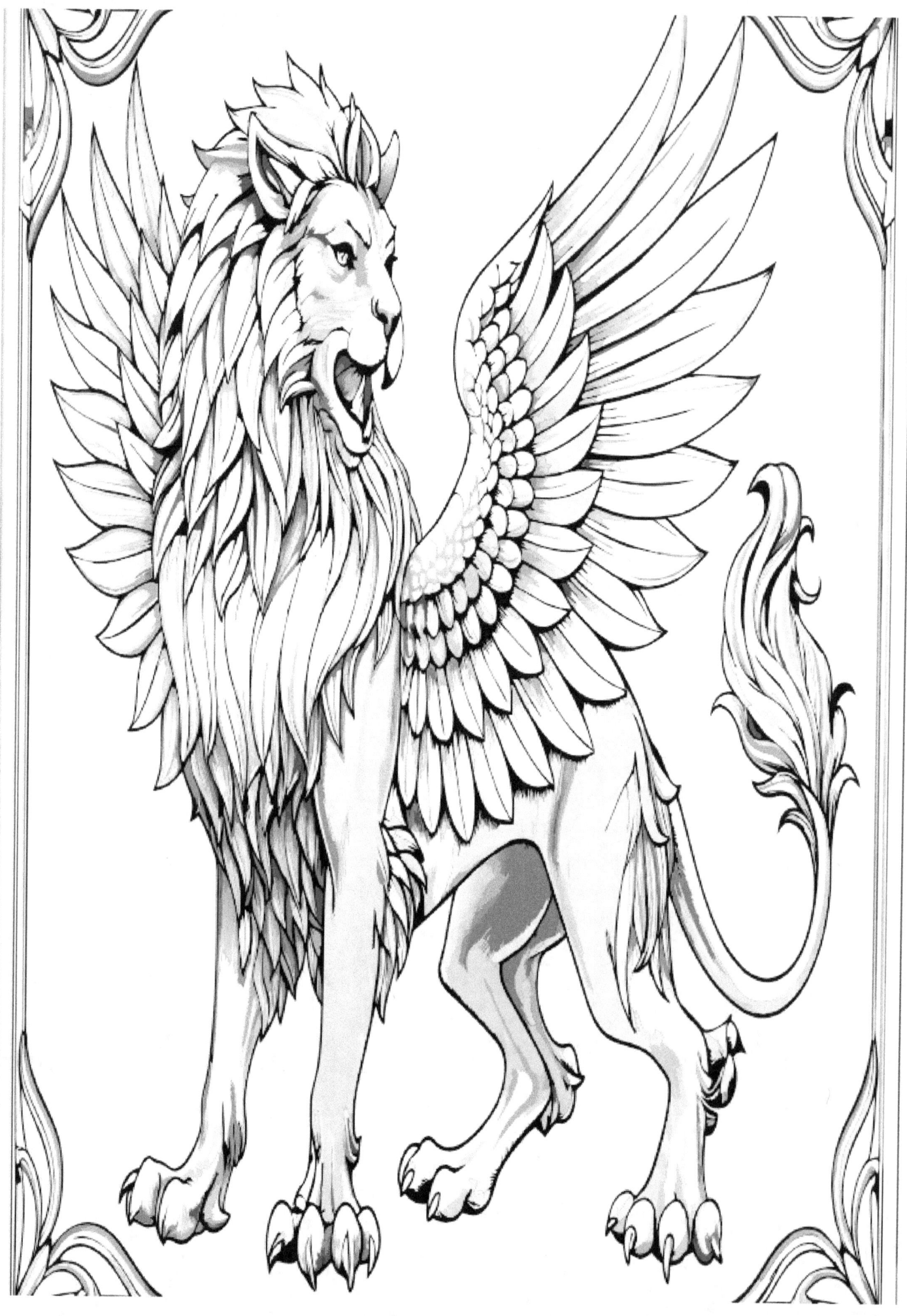

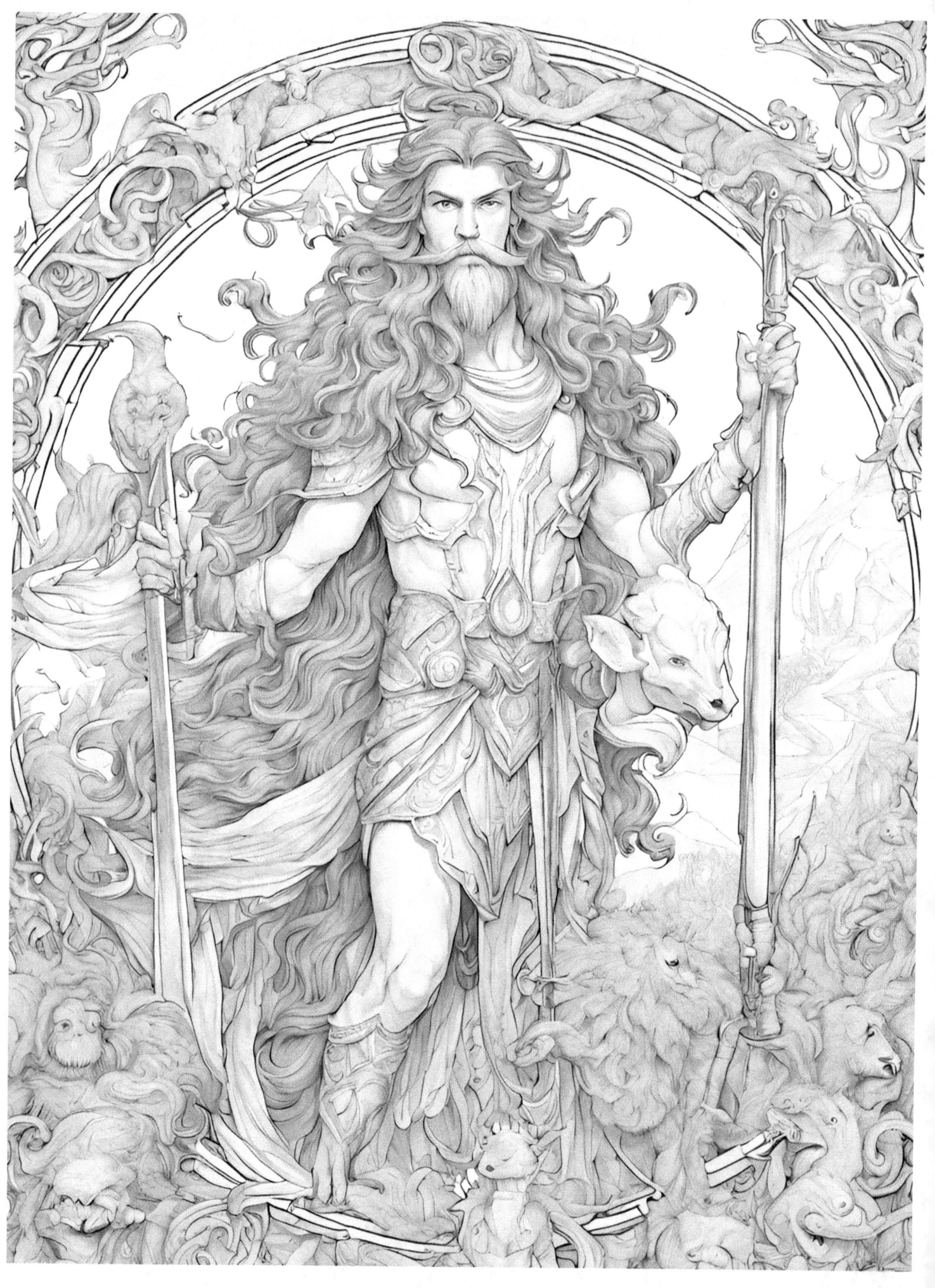

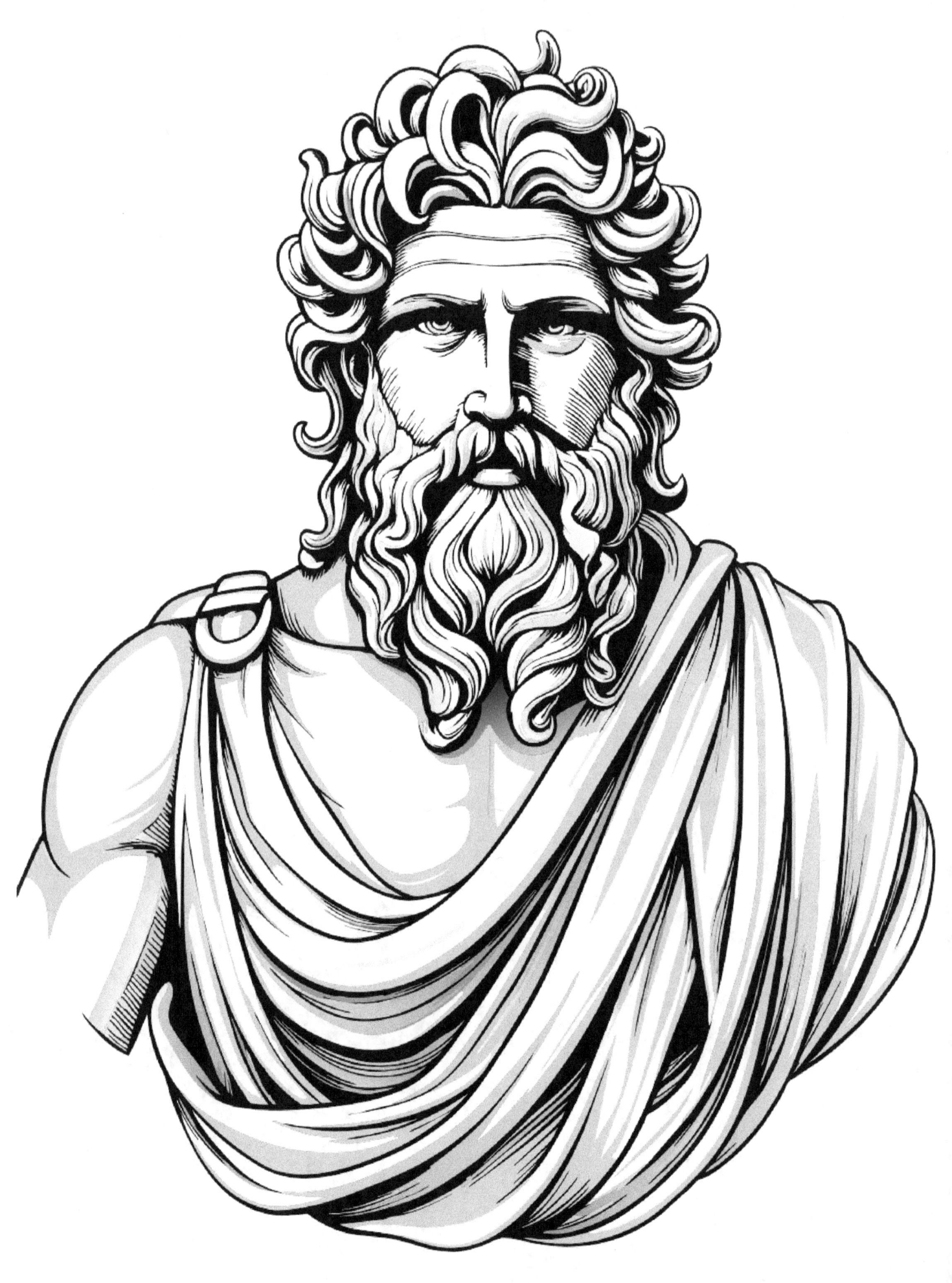

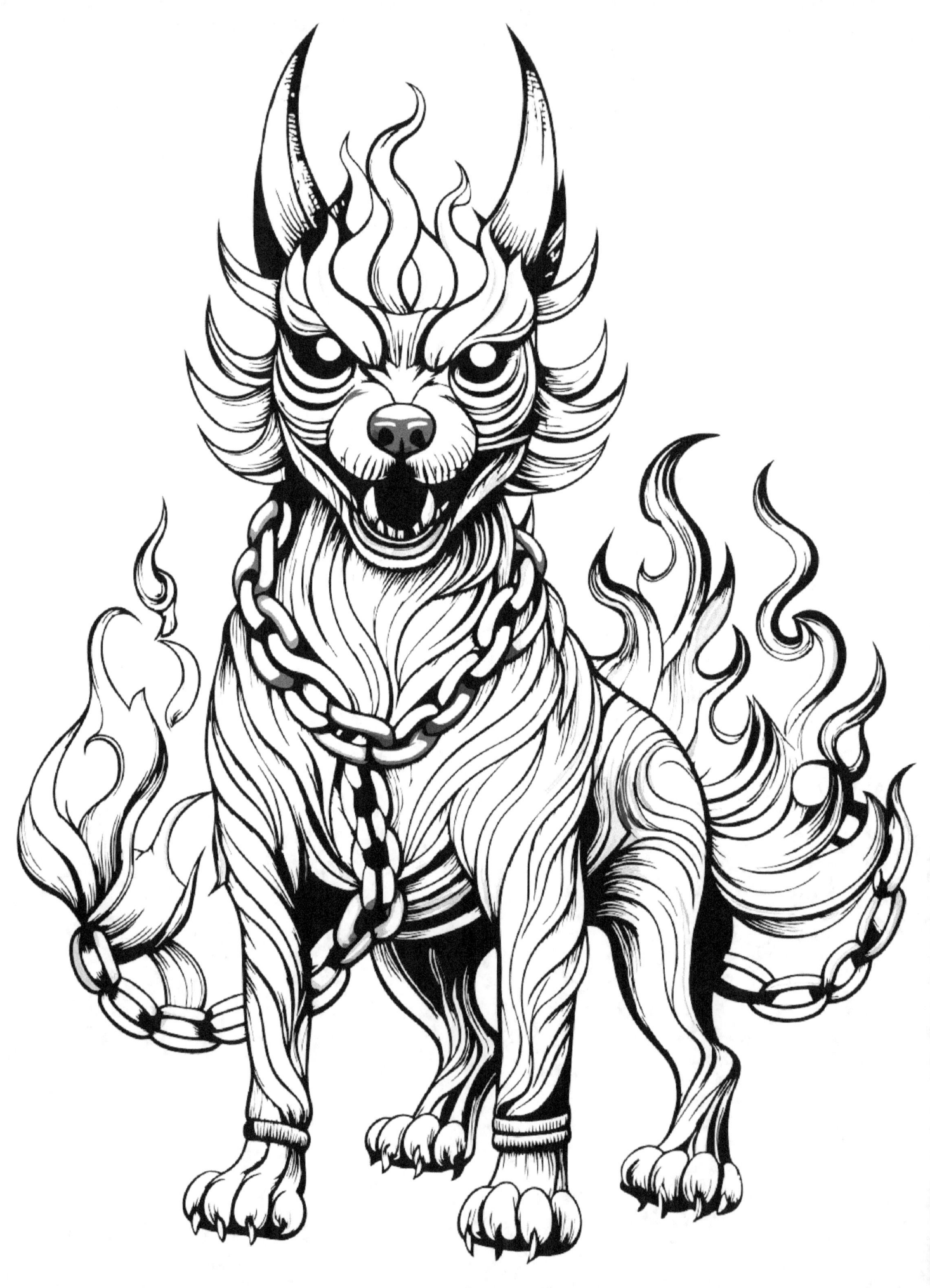

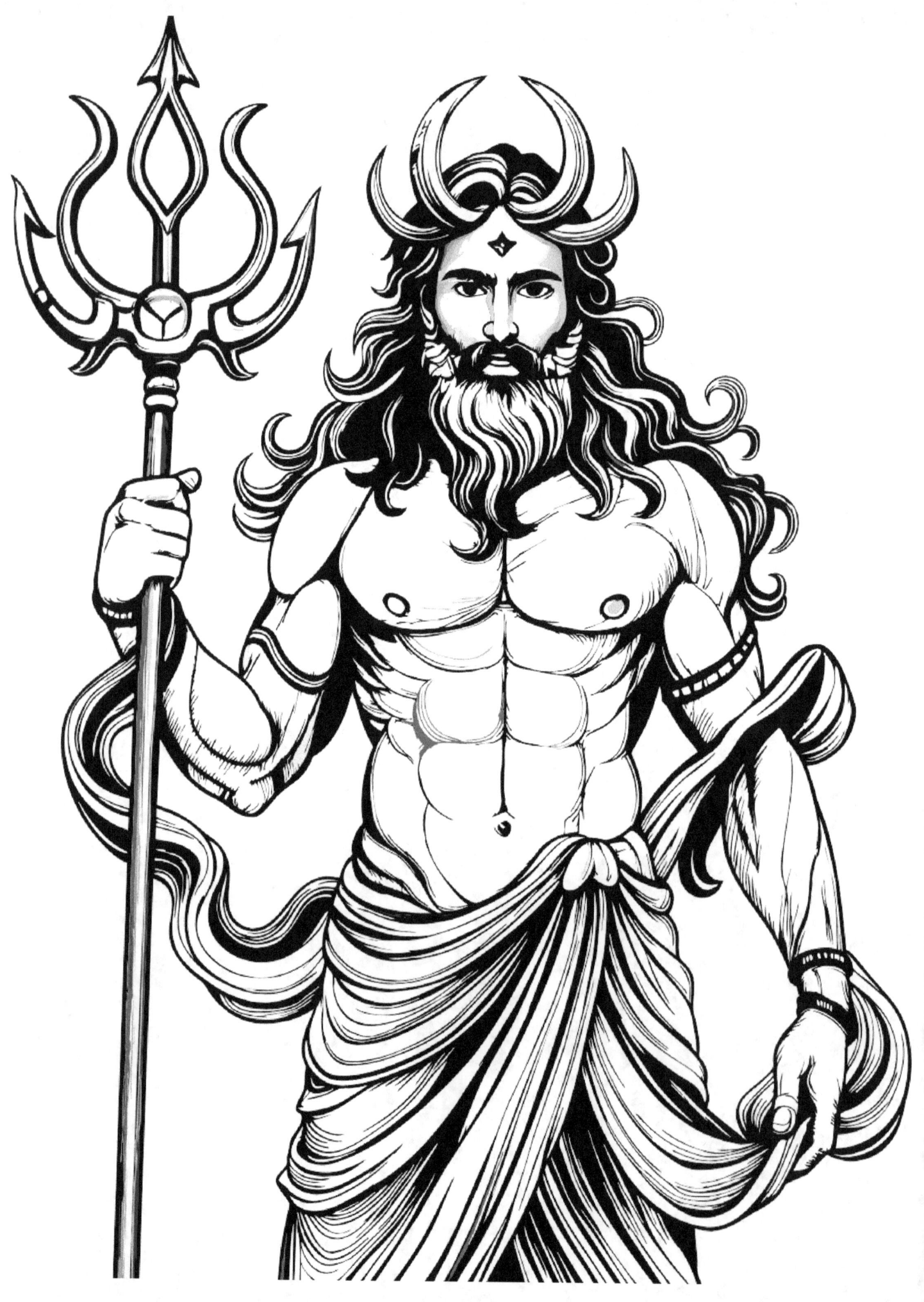

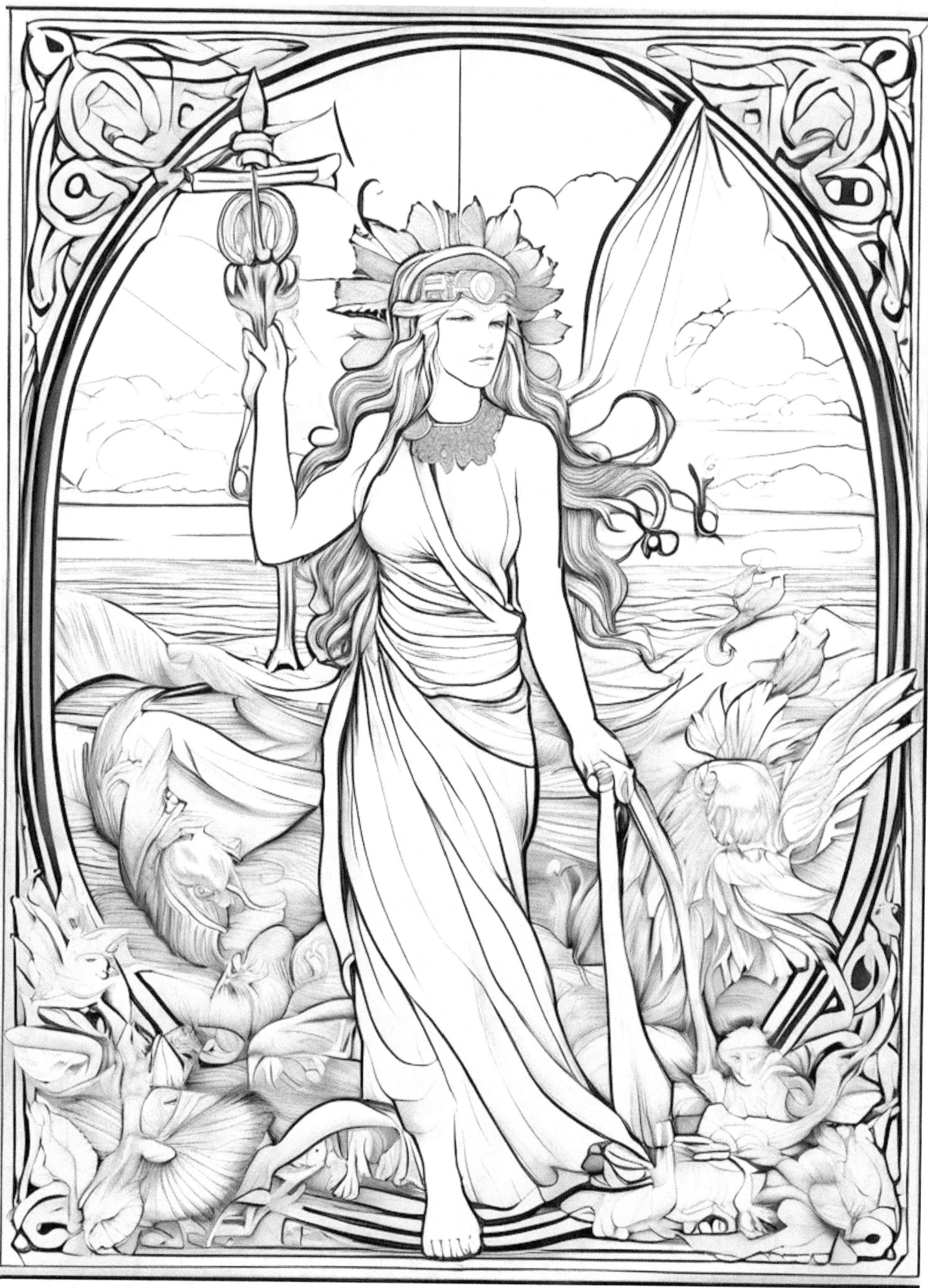

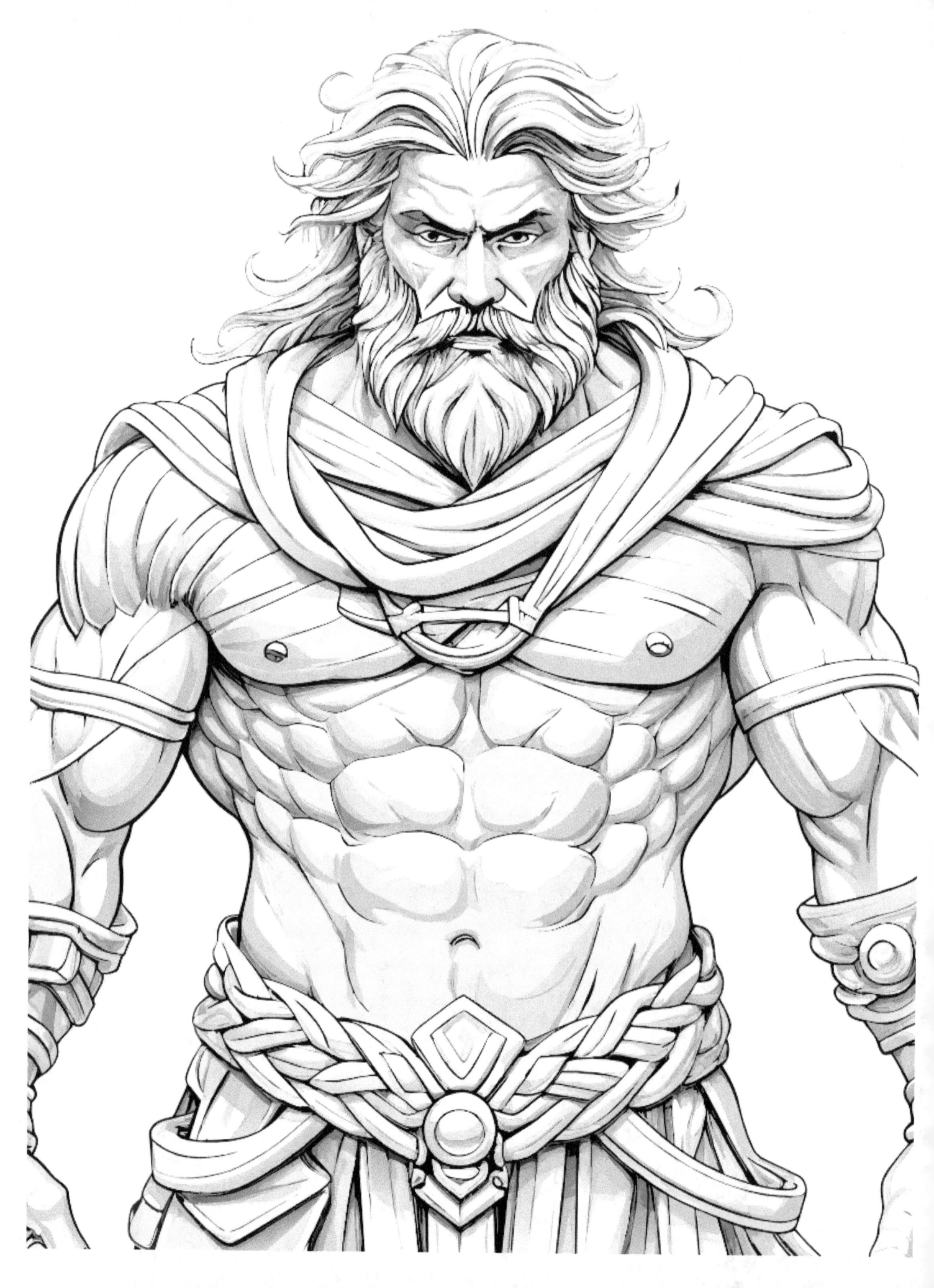